FOREWORD

I do not see my eldest son often because he lives in England. When I do see him we talk a lot, and he likes to hear me talk about the past in Canada as I knew it, and from my angle of vision. This is the angle of a man who had some pretty tough times but managed to survive and is living in reasonable peace and comfort at the age of eighty-five. The last time I was talking with Harry in the garden of my home in Winnipeg, I said to him, "I wish I could put what I've seen in a book, something like those of Jimmy Gray."

Harry said, "Why not? Why don't you write a book?" But I am pretty old and tired, and a letter is about my speed when it comes to writing. My son said, "Look, I'll write the book and you can be the author. You just talk to me, and I'll put it together." And so this is the result of our collaboration. He has written my book for me, and I guess a son cannot do more for a father than that.

Canada as a nation was only twenty-one years old when I was born on the 23rd of July, 1888. Thus my life has covered a good part of the life of the country. I am nearly finished, but the country is still young, and I think it is getting better and stronger. In my experience it has not been an easy country to live in, but it is one worth living in.

Winnipeg,
December, 1975.

Eighty-five Years in Canada

by
S.J.Ferns
&
H.S.Ferns

Queenston House Publishing Co. Ltd.,
102 Queenston Street
Winnipeg, Canada

Grateful acknowledgement is made to the Manitoba Arts Council for a grant to aid in the publication of this book.

Canadian Cataloguing in Publication Data:

Ferns, S.J., 1888—
   Eighty-five years in Canada

ISBN 0-919866-38-7 bd. ISBN 0-919866-39-5 pa.

1. Ferns, S.J., 1888—   I. Ferns, Henry,
1913-   II. Title.

FC27.F47A3   920'.071   C77-000171-8

Printed in Canada by Hignell Printing Limited
Winnipeg, Manitoba

1

I am a Canadian. For most of my life I have taken this for granted. During the past ten years of retirement from active work, however, I have been trying to figure out what this means. A silly thing to think about, perhaps, but there comes a time in the lives of men when they want to know who they are and where they come from; to explain themselves to themselves, to their friends and to the world at large. I have reached the belief that one way of doing this is to give an account of what one has experienced in solving or attempting to solve the problems of living and surviving. To say one is a Canadian, it seems to me, is to say that one has participated, and is participating, in the solution of problems which are both tough and difficult: difficult because of the climate, the distances and the emptiness of the northern part of North America and difficult because the people, apart from the Indians and Eskimoes, have come from all over the world with different languages, different religions and different ways of life.

Experience consists of living and working in a place and not just looking at it. Of course, my experience of Canada has been far from total. I have known only London, Ontario, where I was born and brought up and Canada west of the Great Lakes where I have lived for nearly seventy years and I only know what has happened to me. However, by setting down that experience for others to examine, I may, perhaps, throw some light on the meaning of the assertion "I am a Canadian."

Each Canadian has come from somewhere bringing with him or with her an inheritance of thought, feelings and ways of doing things. But in the main, these have never been as important in shaping people as the hard fact of living in Canada itself. Take the case of my family.

I was born and grew up in a tribe. The Indians are not the only people in Canada who have experienced tribal life. My tribe lived on William Street in London, Ontario. When I tell about myself I cannot escape telling about my grandparents, because they were a continuous and intimate part of my young life, in the way that grandparents have never been for my children. For my children and for my grandchildren, grandparents are visiting people, Christmas people or summer people. For me grandparents really were grand, senior parents—as important or more important—than my physical parents: sources close to hand of authority, love, comfort, trouble and difficulty for my generation as well as for the generation of my parents and uncles and aunts.

The tribe to which I belonged had travelled far. They had found a little land on which to settle and build homes, in a place in Ontario where the deep forests had long since been cut down, the land planted and industry and trading established. And so I want to pick out the individuals of the tribe and say whence they came, starting on my father's side of the family.

My grandfather, John Ferns, came to Canada in 1869. Canada did nothing to him or for him and he did nothing for Canada. On the other hand, my mother's family were transformed within months by coming to Canada. I do not mean that they were miraculously enriched or catastrophically destroyed. Nothing so dramatic as that. In Britain they were servants working for others. Within weeks of arriving in Canada they started building an independent life solidly founded on a small property of their own acquired and developed by hard work.

2

Three of my grandparents were English and one was a Scot. My paternal grandfather was born in Manchester in 1825. Because there is a town of Ferns in County Wexford in Ireland it is sometimes thought that the Ferns to which I belong came from Ireland. If this is so it must have been a long time ago. The name is not very common, and if it is of Irish origin one could suppose that it would occur more often in Ireland than elsewhere. In fact there are fewer Ferns in the Dublin telephone directory than in the telephone directory of London, England, or Toronto, Ontario, or other cities where the name occurs at all. And so I take it that my father was half English and half Scottish.

In 1841 when my grandfather was sixteen or just turned seventeen he enlisted in the East India Company's Infantry. In his pay book he is described as a dyer, and it is easy to believe that he had probably worked several years at this trade by the time he was sixteen or seventeen. He spent fifteen years in India as a soldier, and he was invalided out of the East India Company's service in 1856 shortly before the Indian Mutiny. He seems to have been a good soldier. He was never in trouble, and he left the service with the rank of sergeant major with two campaign medals, some wounds and a mention in despatches. All his life he drew a pension, and I well remember having on many occasions to take my grandfather's warrant for payment to Alderman Cooper in London, in order to have it countersigned by a public official so that payment could be made.

In India my grandfather married a widow, Agnes Lake. Her maiden name was Riddell, and she came of a respectable family of shopkeepers in Glasgow. Apparently her first marriage was a love match, for the story was that when she announced her intention to her parents her mother in a fit of indignation broke a broom stick over her back. Not only was Private Lake a soldier and hence socially contemptible but English and hence politically objectionable. Undeterred, however, Agnes Riddell married her soldier, and accompanied

3

him to India. Her first child was buried at sea off the Cape of Good Hope. Two more died in infancy in India, and her husband either died or was killed in the Sikh Wars.

Her marriage to my grandfather was one of convenience undertaken to make easier her return from India. Private Lake never died in her heart, for there is still in existence a copy of a song in my father's handwriting dated 1872 which she appears to have written concerning a boy in blue whose heart so true continued to beat although buried in a deep grave.

Broken hearted or not my grandmother bore her husband two children, my aunt Mary Ann, born in India and my father Henry Ferns, born in Manchester. Just what my grandfather did in Manchester I never learned. He was a turnkey in Millbank Prison in London, England for a time. In 1869 he decided to migrate to Canada. I do not know what moved him to leave Britain, nor did I ever learn what persuaded him to settle in London, Ontario.

Many years later I read a book about the Roman army. The account of the Roman legions suggested to me a parallel between the life of my grandfather and that of a Roman legionnaire 1700 or 1800 years earlier in history. I could see in my mind's eye a legionnaire who had served the Emperor Trajan on the borders of Egypt living out his life in a small provincial town called Londinium far away from his native Italy. It struck me then that things do not change as much as we may think; and that empires die but the process by which people spread around the world remains the same.

I never remember my grandfather doing any work. I recall him as a man with a white beard, who looked something like George Bernard Shaw, sitting in the summer sun in a Windsor chair with his feet on the rails of the fence around the lawn of his cottage on William Street, London, telling stories about India, or discussing horses about which he had an extensive knowledge or boxing in which he was passionately interested. I can remember with particular vividness the detailed analysis he gave of the qualities and capacities of the contestants in the

4

world heavy weight fight between Fitzsimmons and Corbett in 1897. His prediction with respect to the outcome was wrong.

When he first arrived in London, Grandfather Ferns did work. From 1873 until 1881 he was the sexton of St. Paul's Cathedral. My father used to tell how he and his cousin, Dick Donaghy, the son of my aunt Mary Ann, used to pump the bellows of the organ, presumably at the command of my grandfather. Although he had been a soldier and was used to accepting authority and exercising it himself, he seems to have been a man of awkward, radical and critical temper. He wrote a good hand, and he employed it writing letters critical of society and government. One such letter caused him to lose the office of sexton. In it he suggested that one of the clergy was too liberally using the communion wine for non-sacramental purposes. Given the strength of the teetotal sentiment in London this was a very damaging allegation, and the vestry dispensed with my grandfather's services.

Whether he was cruel with my grandmother I do not know. He was certainly authoritarian, and she seemed always to fear him. From time to time he used to upbraid her, and she would stand before him with both hands raised as if to ward off a blow, but at the same time she chattered at him in Hindi giving him a piece of her mind in a language which she spoke but no one else could understand. Although they inhabited together a cottage two doors away from our family home on William Street, Grandfather and Grandmother Ferns lived separate lives. Grandfather Ferns, for example, always ate alone and in a peculiar way. I never saw him eat anything but bread. Each day he procured a large loaf of coarse bread which he cut into cubes with a clasp knife. These cubes he dipped one by one in strong tea before popping them into his mouth. His other nourishment consisted of spirits which he drew from a barrel. He was never a drunkard, and I never once saw him even slightly tipsy. Spirits were simply part of his diet taken with a view to sustenance and nothing more. Eccentric as his eating habits were by the standards of Ontario, they

5

were probably the result of his military training and service.

What Granny Ferns managed to obtain beyond the essentials of bread and tea I do not know. In my home we always ate our dinner in the middle of the day. Very often before sitting down to our meal one of my brothers or sisters or I was sent off to Granny Ferns with a plate of hot roast meat, potatoes and vegetables folded in a napkin. Her conception of luxurious hospitality was to offer a guest bread buttered on both sides. Often on a cold winter evening I used to drop into her cottage after delivering newspapers, which I did from the age of ten; Granny Ferns always offered me a cup of tea with the same words. "Take this, Bub. It will warm the cockles of your heart." And it did.

Granny Ferns was a small woman who grew smaller as she grew older. Once every week she wrapped herself in a black shawl, put on a black bonnet tied under her chin, and set off down William Street towards the Thames. She crossed by the Blackfriars bridge into London West, and there spent the day with her daughter, Mary Ann Donaghy. She was a quiet, self-contained woman of great sweetness of disposition, and I remember her with affection and respect. She died in the same month as Queen Victoria.

The cottage in which Grandfather and Grandmother Ferns lived was austere and bare. It left the impression of being clean, swept out and unfurnished. The ex-soldier and his wife seemed to have created in a cottage on William Street in London, Ontario the atmosphere of a barracks in India. Two teak chests stood in the hallway, and in these their worldly possessions were stowed away. There were tables and chairs and a bed. The only decoration on the walls were framed campaign medals: two of my grandfather's and one of my grandmother's.

Impervious as my Grandfather Ferns seems to have been to surrounding influences, and indifferent as he was to the example of society in the place where he had settled, he none the less yielded in an extraordinary way to the attractions of advertising. Being a great reader of newspapers he came upon a proposition which held promise of introducing into his cottage a refinement of civilization in the shape of a secretary: an article of furniture which combined in one unit a bookshelf, a desk and a chest of drawers. To obtain a secretary one was invited to sell a great quantity of yellow laundry soap, the salesman achieving the quota being rewarded with a secretary free of all charges. Selling soap was beneath the dignity of my Grandfather Ferns. He bypassed this operation by purchasing the required quantity of soap for his own use. Henceforward his cottage was not only a dwelling place but a soap warehouse. For several years after his death my mother was still using the laundry soap which constituted a major part of the family inheritance.

Grandfather Ferns was younger than his wife, and he survived her for a few years. When she died, Grandpa went into an old folks' home. This did not seem right to my parents. In the old folks' home someone stole the old man's campaign medals, and so he returned to William Street. He sat yarning in the sun for another summer and then died.

My mother's name was Hannah Dickens. Her father Rowland Dickens (it infuriated him to see his name spelt Roland) was born in 1829 at Teigh in the county of Rutland in England. Teigh was, and is, a very small village lost amid great fields mostly given over to cereal grains and root crops. Teigh consists of a few cottages, a small church, and a large elegant vicarage built in the eighteenth century by a man who was both a vicar and a lord in that part of the world. The church is something of a curiosity. The congregation sit facing each other across a central aisle to the altar. At the end of the church opposite the altar is a system of hidden stairways leading to a desk at one level where the priest appears like a cuckoo in a cuckoo clock to read the lesson and to a pulpit at a higher level from which the sermon is preached.

My grandfather Dickens came of a well-to-do family in Rutlandshire. His father died early in life, and this had a great

7

effect upon my grandfather's future. His mother was a very quarrelsome and difficult woman who refused, and in the end was denied, all assistance by her husband's family. In order to maintain her independence, she kept a small shop and post office. Two of her sons enlisted in the British Army and were killed in the Crimean War. Her third son, my grandfather, was turned down for military service on account of an ulcerated varicose vein, which troubled him all his life. He entered the domestic service of a landed family with estates in Rutland and Lincolnshire: the Heathcotes, whose most distinguished forebear was a Lord Mayor of London and one of the founders of the Bank of England. During my grandfather's service the head of the family was raised from a baronet to baron with the title of Lord Aveland. My grandfather seems to have flourished in the service of the Heathcotes, for he became a butler and he learned much. Lady Aveland was a great gardener, and she used to insist on being attended by Dickens to whom she taught gardening with some effect. Years later in Ontario people came from all over London to see my grandfather Dickens' garden where he grew vegetables, fruits and flowers in great profusion, all tastefully arranged for utility and beauty.

My grandfather Dickens married Mary Barrett, born in the considerable Rutlandshire village of Ketton near Stamford, the ninth and last child of a strongly evangelical family. The head of the family was a man reputed for his good works and his close attention to the great preachers of his day. He once walked thirty miles to hear the young Spurgeon preach the Word.

Mary Barrett became a lady's maid in the service of the Heathcote family. A tale was told of a romance between my grandmother and a son of the family. He was wounded in the Crimean War and died shortly after returning home. Even if a Russian bullet had not ended the affair it is safe to assume that Mary would never have been able to cross the barriers of class, and that she did as well as could be expected by marrying the butler, which she did at St. George's, Hanover Square, in old London (as the people of my London always referred to the capital city of the United Kingdom).

Shortly after his marriage my grandfather Dickens became the keeper of a public house in Oakham, the county town of Rutland, where my mother was born in 1862. Six children were born of my Dickens grandparents of whom three survived: my mother, my uncle Joe Dickens and my aunt Lily. My grandfather did not last long as a publican. Whether he consumed too much of the substance of the enterprise or allowed his guests to consume too much on credit, is not clear. The first possibility seems to be the most likely. In Canada my grandfather Dickens was never a drinking man and his exploits as a drinker were limited to the times when he went to the Englishman's Picnic at Port Stanley on Lake Erie whence on more than one occasion he returned in a horse cab the worse for wear. Although he worked too hard ever to have a drinking problem, there must have been a time in his life when his family learned a fear of drinking and this seems to have been the origin of my mother's rigid and almost fanatical teetotalism.

After his failure as a publican, my grandfather moved to Burton-on-Trent where he was employed by a firm of brewers, Inde Coope. There he and his wife resolved to emigrate. Grandmother Dickens had two brothers who had gone to Australia. They wrote encouraging reports of opportunities in Queensland, and urged their sister and family to follow them. In 1871 the decision was made. My grandfather seems not to have lost the regard of his first employer, who offered to assist him in emigration. All was prepared for departure when a letter arrived to say that depression had set in Australia, and emigration was not advisable. My grandparents decided not to unpack, but to migrate to Canada, about which they appear to have known little.

When they arrived in Quebec, people there advised them to "go west". It might be supposed that this meant go to Manitoba, lately become a province of the new Dominion of Canada. This was not the case. At that time "go west" meant to go to Canada West, recently renamed Ontario. My grandparents

9

looked at a map, and resolved not to go too far west because they did not wish to be too close to the republican United States. They fixed on Strathroy, Ontario, as a spot sufficiently far from the Yankees to ensure their safety and well-being. On the train from Quebec, however, they met a man who advised them that Strathroy was no place to settle, but that London was, on account of its size—about 28,000—and its employment opportunities. The man himself was a foreman in the car shops of the Grand Trunk Railway in London, and he promised my grandfather a job.

When Rowland Dickens arrived in his new home on the banks of the Thames in Ontario he ceased to be a butler, a publican or a brewery worker. He became a laborer. This is how he is described in the first contract he made in Canada on 15 January 1872: a contract with John Williams, esquire, to purchase for $150, 8,500 square feet of land on William Street between Piccadilly Street and Pall Mall Street. For this land he paid $15.00 in cash and $135.00 by mortgage to be discharged in five years. This was the first of several land purchases made by my grandfather during his life time, all but one of them for the purpose of providing space on which to build houses for his family.

At the time when Grandfather Dickens purchased this land, London was beginning to expand from its nucleus at the junction of the north and south forks of the river, called the Askunesippi by the Indians, the La Tranche by the French, and the Thames by the first lieutenant governor of Upper Canada, John Graves Simcoe. In 1872 William Street was more a mark on a surveyor's map than a street lined with houses. The forest had been cut down, and the land had the appearance of a flat plain. If, today, William Street is a well treed avenue, it is because the people who built their cottages as my grandfather did planted trees in front of their homes. A great tree still stands in front of 715 William Street which my grandfather planted over a century ago, and it is but one of the many splendid trees which others planted in the late 1860's and the 1870's.

My grandfather purchased his land when it was frozen and buried in snow. When spring came he discovered that water coursed through one end of it flowing away to the south west across land on Miles Street which ran parallel to William Street. For some years until the water was put underground in sewers grandfather Dickens regularly received a lawyer's letter from his neighbour on Miles Street requiring him to stop the water on his land flowing on to her land. As regularly as he received the letters he threw them away unanswered.

The life that my Dickens grandparents developed was one in which traditional rural work was joined with industrial city work. Both Grandpa and Granny Dickens worked in order to earn money, but both worked hard at providing for themselves and their family by growing and preserving food. Grandpa Dickens worked for many years in the car shops as a general laborer. In the evenings and at weekends he worked for Sir John Carling, a celebrated brewer and Member of Parliament whose name has gone around the world on beer labels and in advertisements. He looked after Sir John's garden and his furnace, and did the same for another gentleman named Major Beattie, who lived on Dundas Street. And then he tended his own garden and fruit trees. When one considers that he was obliged to rise before six o'clock every morning in order to walk several miles to the car shops where work began at 7 a.m., and then walked home in the evening to another half day of work, much of it physical and strenuous, one marvels at his energy and fortitude. It is possible to regard his life as a triumph, but he did not so regard it himself. Not infrequently he was heard muttering to himself as he walked "What a fool I have been! What a fool I have been!"

My grandmother Dickens was likewise an earner of money. She had an attractive personality, a wide variety of talents and a capacity for selfless devotion to a task in hand which evoked admiration from the beneficiaries of her care. Because she had experience of the social graces and practices of the British aristocracy, she was employed from time to time by the aspiring

11

bourgeoisie of London to arrange their houses for evening parties. She performed this service for Sir John Carling, and my mother used to tell how as a young girl she accompanied her mother to the Carling home where Sir John commended her for her manners and appearance and gave her ten cents.

Granny Dickens moved easily and confidently among all kinds and conditions of people, and she performed for them a great variety of services which nowadays are the province of specialists: nurses, doctors, undertakers and social workers. She was a practical nurse, and a midwife. She laid out the dead and assisted at funeral arrangements. She covered the whole range of human experience from birth to death, and was as much skilled in preparing a wedding party as a wake.

Granny Dickens retained to the end of her days many of the characteristics formed by her early life in old rural England: a matter of fact frankness about birth, procreation and death about which there could be no concealment and about which there need be no discussion. At the same time she had an earnest and unquestioning religious faith which expressed itself in unselfish good works undertaken without any special moral effort. These two characteristics of my granny Dickens which set her somewhat apart from the average Londoner of that time can be illustrated by two stories about her.

The first concerned nursing the widow of a steam boat captain who was dying of cancer. This poor woman was in great pain and she lingered too long in the world. Granny Dickens attended her with the greatest of care in a physical sense and somehow brought her comfort in her distress and loneliness. One day not long before she died, the woman asked Granny what was her religion. She replied that she was C. of E. in the matter-of-fact and almost dismissive way the English have of referring to their faith. The woman then said that the religion which produced Granny Dickens must be the true religion of God, and that she wished to be received into the Church of England. The vicar of the Cronyn Memorial Church, a friend of Granny's, was sent for, and the widow of the steamboat captain was baptized in the Anglican faith and then died.

The second also concerned a death. Granny had just finished laying out the corpse of a well known citizen of London who was a very small man. I was then a small boy, perhaps five or six years old, and I was present with Granny when she and some other women were gossiping about the deceased. His small stature was remarked upon, whereupon Granny said, "Well, Tommy may have been a small man, but he had the biggest tool I ever saw in my life." There was a great laugh, but I could not understand why. I asked my brother Rolly, who was four years older than I, what was so funny, and he explained to me why everyone laughed at something which did not seem to me amusing or even comprehensible.

This must have happened in 1893 or1894. In those days the matter-of-fact candour about the facts of life and death displayed by my Granny Dickens was not much liked, and this remained so for most of my life. There has, however, been a great change latterly in public attitude in this respect. Recently I read a novel, *Surfacing*, by a woman named Margaret Atwood. One of my grandsons, who teaches in a university in eastern Canada, is of the opinion that Miss Atwood is one of the most talented writers in Canada. From her picture on the dust jacket of her book she looks to be a decent, attractive and intelligent young woman. And yet she puts into the mouths of her characters, both men and women, words like "fuck". For most of my life this was considered one of the very worst of the four letter words, so bad, indeed, that synonyms like "screw" or "have a piece of tail" were invented to replace it.

When I was young, boys and men had a rude language of their own: a combination of obscenity and blasphemy. I began to learn this language when I was about six, and I understood, or thought I understood, it all by the time I was eleven or twelve years old. Vulgar language seemed both sinful and manly. One sometimes felt uncomfortable and conscience stricken about using it. Some boys and men used it all the time, and larded every sentence with dirty, blasphemous words of every kind, but these boys or men tended to be looked down on as foul-mouthed. On the other hand boys or men who never used vulgar language were regarded as sissies. In fact there were few boys or men who did not understand and use the secret vocabulary of coarseness and blasphemy.

Dirty, blasphemous talk was never used in one's home or before one's family. I never knew a family who allowed such talk in the family home, or any boy whose father would not give him a beating if he used rude and blasphemous words in front of his mother or sisters. It was even dangerous to use the secret vocabulary of men with one's own father even though he himself might use such language among his friends. One never used four letter words in the presence of girls. Although a few girls might know coarse words, I do not think there were many who did. When I grew up and discovered that some women did not mind hearing or telling a smutty story, this was not really acceptable, and to hear or tell a smutty story tended to establish for a woman a less than admirable character.

My purpose in reflecting, thus, on one of the changes in our talk and our manners is to suggest that my Granny Dickens was a different kind of person from the norm of her time and place: more earthy, more honest and more religious, but also unlike anyone I ever encounter nowadays when what was normal in Canadian society at the turn of the century has long since passed away.

My Ferns grandparents led separate lives much like, I suppose, sergeants lead lives separate from privates in an army. My Dickens grandparents were separate in a different way. They both worked hard, and they both earned money. Just as both sought to be independent of the rest of the world through possessing a patch of earth of their own, they each sought some kind of independence of each other. In my Granny Dicken's case she tried to accumulate small sums of money of her own, and Grandpa Dickens was forever seeking to merge her money in the family stock of savings which he controlled. Granny hid her money, and Grandpa tried to find it. When Granny was absent from their cottage and curiosity and the hunting instinct got the upper hand in Grandpa, he would turn over everything in the house in his search for his wife's treasure. My sister, Marjorie, tells of how one day Granny Dickens came into our house in great indignation. "Dickens has been through the house again!" she declared.

Granny Dicken's religion helped her to preserve the secrecy of her hoard, but not in the way one might expect. Grandfather Dickens was an agnostic, not given to discussing his views, but firm in his determination to have nothing to do with churches, clergymen and their superstitions. Granny Dickens, therefore, secreted her bank notes between the leaves of her Bible, certain in the knowledge that her husband's faith would prevent him from investigating hers. And so it turned out that she was able to satisfy the spark of independence which in her, was symbolised by a few bank notes hidden in her Bible.

My Dickens grandparents lived to a good age. One died in 1913: the other in 1917.

2

Although my parents were born in England, they received much of their education in Canada. At the age of nine my father was sent to the Grammar School on King Street, and my mother attended St. George's School on Waterloo Street. At fourteen my father was apprenticed to the printing trade, with the London Printing and Lithographing Company, which produced the *Farmers Advocate*, catalogues and calendars. He learned lithography, type setting and the operation of printing machines. His specialty was presses and what was known as "three colour work" required for the printing of calendars, then and for many years a favourite form of advertising by merchants, manufacturers, banks and commercial houses. When the automatic feeding of paper into the presses came in, my father mastered the intricacies of the new machines to such an extent that he was offered the post of field representative of the Miehle Company of Chicago, one of the two big manufacturers of advanced printing machinery. But my mother was opposed to this, and perhaps he was, too. He remained in the employ of the London Printing and Lithographing Company for 54 years until his death in 1928.

As children my parents lived within a hundred yards of one another on William Street. They were married in 1881, and moved into a cottage which my grandfather Dickens built for them next door to his on the land purchased in 1872. Two cottages on the frontage possessed by Grandpa Dickens was a tight fit, and the home of the newly married couple was right on the property line of the adjoining house. By a stroke of luck the owner of the adjoining property decided to move not only himself but his cottage away from William Street. The cottage was jacked up on skids and towed away by six powerful horses, and my Grandfather Dickens made an offer for ten feet of the now vacant property. This was accepted. For some reason the adjoining property was of greater depth than my grandfather's with the result that there was a little enclave measuring 10 feet by 25 feet at the bottom of the garden. There my Grandfather Dickens had one of the most abundant raspberry patches I have ever encountered.

My parents had six children. All grew up and all have lived more than seventy-five years. Their eldest child, Edith, is still (1974) alive in Windsor, Ontario, aged 92. My elder brothers lived to the ages of 81 and 85, and my younger sisters are alive. At the time of my 50th wedding anniversary in 1963 we all six of us were alive, and our combined ages exceeded 450 years.

Perhaps at this stage I should say something briefly about what luck and effort produced for my brothers and sisters. My two brothers went to the United States early in life, and became American citizens. The eldest was Henry Roland. I always liked Rolly, but there was something odd and unsatisfactory about him; a kind of timidity and incapacity to settle down. He was intelligent enough, and he was a great reader, but only of newspapers. He had what was known as a "good head for figures", and, after briefly serving an apprenticeship as a cigar maker, he took an "office job", and became a bookkeeper and accountant. To him New York was the centre of the universe, and the goal of his dreams. He worked as an accountant in several large American cities. He was briefly married, and he was employed as an auditor of passenger accounts by the Michigan Central Railroad in Chicago when the crash came in 1929. Like ten million or so other Americans, Rolly lost his job and all his savings in 1930 or thereabouts. Until this time he had been a quite fanatical partisan of the Republican Party, but the New Deal social assistance programme turned him round politically so that Franklin Roosevelt became for him a species of savior. Eventually he found a job as an accountant handyman with a crippled watchmaker who kept a small shop in the Loop in Chicago. Rolly worked for the watchmaker until he died in 1966 without sufficient resources to pay for his own funeral. Along the way he had become a Roman Catholic and the only person who visited him in his last illness was a Catholic priest. For three years before he died he confidently predicted that the letter he was writing to me was his last, and so when he did really write me his last letter I was unaware of his condition. I still feel broken-hearted that I did not visit him before he died.

My other brother, John Shipley, was a successful man. I never knew Jack very well, and for half a century I never saw him at all. He too had "a head for figures", and could add four columns of numbers in a single operation. He won medals at school. He entered the office of the London Printing and Lithographing Company, but before he was 21 he held a well paid, responsible post with a firm of shoe manufacturers. When this business was taken over by a large American company just before the first World War, Jack went to the United States where he worked for a gas company in Detroit, and then for Palmolive-Peet, the well known soap manufacturers. He was sent by this firm to California. Although Jack was an intelligent, shrewd and disciplined man, he was not all ambition. Because he liked living in California, he turned down an opportunity to work in the head office of the Palmolive organization in New York, where he might well have risen to the top of one of the big American business enterprises. As it was he remained the auditor of the western region of the company for the rest of his working life. He was a prominent member of the Masonic Order in California, and when he was the Senior Warden of one of the Lodges he admitted to the Order Earl Warren, later Governor of California and Chief Justice of the United States. Jack married a London girl, and they had a daughter comparatively late in life. He was living with his daughter and her husband, a civilian administrator in the U.S. Naval Hospital at Bethesda, Maryland, when he died in 1972.

My sisters all married, and remained in Ontario. Edith, the eldest, married a mechanic in a shoe factory named Roland Burton. He was also a part time musician who played the cornet in several popular dance bands. Edith and her husband and two daughters lived in Ontario towns like Brantford and Belleville and finally for many years in Windsor. My sister Gladys married a brass worker named Roy Walters, and all her married life she lived less than half a mile from the home on William Street where she was born. My sister Marjorie, who was the youngest by five years, has lived all her life in London. She married a man of German extraction from Kitchener, Stewart Olheiser. He was badly gassed in World War 1. After leaving the Canadian Army he became an X-ray technologist who developed several devices for taking X-ray photographs. He lived in constant expectation of dying from the effects of gas. In fact he lived to a reasonable age, and died from the cumulative effects of over-exposure to X-rays.

As for me, I was born on 23 July, 1888, the third son and fourth child. I cannot believe there was anything very exceptional about my childhood. Although my mother was inclined to be ill-tempered and bossy, I have no recollection of cruelty or oppression, or of any special happiness stemming from family life. If anything I was allowed too much freedom, and, as shall emerge, I was managed with short-sighted carelessness. I mention my mother first because she was more ever-present in the lives of us children than our father. He was a small quiet man, who, for as long as I can remember, was very deaf. My mother believed he had wax in his ears, and attributed his deafness to a stubborn and stupid refusal to have a doctor clean out his ears. An alternative explanation, which he offered, was the noisy nature of his work among moving machinery in the presence of which he could hear better than most people. We now know that he had otiosclerosis, which, skipping a generation, was inherited by both my sons, who have escaped the silence, suffering and misunderstanding of my father by the surgical installation of plastic replacement parts in their ears.

A factor in the comparative dominance of my mother in our home life was the long hours my father worked. I never remember my father working less than sixty hours a week, and sometimes he brought lithographic work home with him. His absorption in his work was total. His only recreation was fishing, and he did this, I think, because, sitting on the end of the pier at Port Stanley, he found relief from the hay fever which afflicted him in August and September every year. He left gardening and domestic chores to Grandfather Dickens. When he was not working on a lithographic plate, he spent his time in a chair smoking his pipe and reading the newpapers. On Saturday nights he always brought home the weekend edition of the *Buffalo Express* which kept him occupied on Sundays.

During most of my years at home my father was paid $9.00 for his sixty hours of work each week. He used to bring home his pay in a sealed envelope and give it to my mother. She used to open it and pour the one dollar bills into her lap, and would caress them with a sort of sensuous touch of her fingers. She kept everything except for a pittance which she allowed to her husband for a package of Tuckett's Pipe Tobacco and a plug of MacDonald's Chewing Tobacco. The pipe tobacco was for home consumption, and the chewing tobacco was for work. Like most printers my father chewed tobacco while he worked.

Even when T-bone steak was two pounds for a quarter (25 cents) and sausages were a nickel (5 cents) a pound, $9.00 was not much for the keep of a family, which, by 1895, numbered eight people not to mention my Granny Ferns who was helped in one way or another. The real family income was, however, greater than $9.00 a week. The working men of London could never have lived and raised families on what the employers paid them in those days. They were able to get by and even to prosper because many of them—most of them in my recollection—had their plots of land where they grew food eaten fresh in summer and preserved in winter. Of course they bought from the farmers who offered their produce for sale on the Covent

Garden Market in London three days a week; and sugar, salt, spices and dried druits from grocers. But the working man's wife was a food processer, canner and preserver, and her husband was still a small farmer as well as a wage laborer.

If the husband earned money so did the children. My brothers and I "carried papers". I became a young business man at the age of ten: buying, delivering and selling newspapers.

In London at that time there were several possibilities open to the aspiring paper boy. He could deliver papers to homes or he could sell directly on the street. There were two major newspapers: the *London Free Press* which was the Tory paper and the *London Advertiser* which was Grit. No one in those days ever spoke of Conservatives or Liberals. There was a third paper *The News*, but it was of little account, and disappeared. I chose to deliver the *London Free Press* rather than the *Tizer* not because I was a Tory, for being Protestants, I suppose we were Tories, but because I could make more money with the *Free Press*. It came out in two editions, morning and evening. For delivering twenty-five to thirty papers each morning one received $1.25 a week. This was a fixed sum, and the $1.25 was a kind of wage. In the evening, however, the *Free Press* sold the papers to the boys for a ½ cent each, and the boys sold them for 1 cent either directly on the street or 6 cents a week delivered at the home. The morning delivery was easier in as much as one received a flat rate and the papers were ready in a bundle when one arrived at the newspaper office about 6 a.m. The evening delivery involved a competitive struggle, with cash on the counter, in order to get one's papers soon enough to deliver one's merchandise before the evening meal. On the other hand one could build up a big route. I built mine up to fifty customers. On average I managed to gross $2.00 - $3.00 a week. Considering I worked about 24 - 25 hours a week I earned about 10 - 12 cents an hour at a time when my father, a highly skilled man, was earning 15 cents an hour.

Some parents took all their children's earnings. Mine did

not. I was expected to buy all my outer clothing: suits, over-coat, trousers and shoes. My parents provided me with under-wear, and linen, and my Granny Dickens knitted my stockings and mended them. Mine were the costly items. But I had money to spend as I pleased. In the course of time I bought myself a watch and eventually a bicycle. Both of these were necessary working capital in my business, but they were also articles for which I longed and their possession gave me great pleasure and prestige. I never felt poor. On the contrary I always had money to spend. On Christmas Eve I came home with a pocket full of quarters given me by my customers, and I was able to buy Christmas presents for my family and something for myself. I cannot say that earning money at an early age ever produced in me a talent for capitalist profit making, but it did teach me the relationship between working and spending, which on the whole I liked doing. I never became obsessed with accumulating money. I had a sort of negative obsession. I dreaded being in debt, and I loved to pay cash for things I wanted even when I was a small boy.

Like my mother I attended St. George's School. School and I did not agree. I often found excuses to beg off going there, and I played hookey when I could. Arithmetic and numbers work I hated, but I liked history and composition, which involved learning to write English prose. Mainly, how-ever, I disliked discipline and being confined in a school room. One teacher tried firm, physical discipline with me when I was about ten years old or so, and I kicked her with such effect that I was transferred out of her care. One teacher I remember with affection and respect, an austere grey maiden lady named Miss Althouse. I think she taught me more than the rest of the teachers combined.

My school career came to an end when I was in the eighth grade, the last year before going on to the High School. I was not yet thirteen years of age. It happened like this in 1901 not long after the death of Queen Victoria.

I had a chum, George Prodgers. George was a big red-headed youngster who on account of his freckled face looked as if he had sneezed in a bran mash. George was very strong. He liked fighting and he nearly always won. The Principal of St. George's School, Mr. Samuel Baker, did not like fighting, and he was determined to stamp it out. To this end he patrolled the school yard armed with a heavy, hardwood pointer, the instrument of public peace. When one day at recess Mr. Baker encountered George Prodgers fighting, he assumed that he was was the aggressor, and proceeded to belabor him with the heavy pointer. This stopped the fight, but it left some marks on George's person.

Now George Prodger's father was a big strong man who worked as a locomotive engineer on the railway. This was a very prestigious employment. Having viewed his son's bruises Mr. Prodgers visited Mr. Baker and proceeded to give the Principal a taste of the medicine with which George had been treated. In the process Mr. Prodgers broke Mr. Baker's glasses.

Mr. Baker then laid charges of assault and battery against Mr. Prodgers. Mr. Prodgers was arrested and summoned to appear before the Police Magistrate.

It was at this stage that I entered the drama. I was called as a witness for the defence. I had no hesitation in bearing witness for a chum against the cruel tyranny of the Principal of St. George's School. This ended my school career, for I resolved never to enter St. George's School again, a wise decision perhaps because Mr. Baker was my teacher in Grade Eight.

Not so wise was the decision to abandon education altogether. I have referred to the careless, short sighted liberality of my parents' management of their children, at least in my case. They could easily have asked for me to be transferred to Princess Avenue School. Better they could have forbidden me to get involved in the affair of Rex vs. Prodgers in the London Police Court. I can now see that complete freedom accorded a boy in his thirteenth year is irresponsible idiocy, but I was given my freedom and that is how I used it. One of the main themes of my life henceforward was the round about way—the

23

hard way—I obtained an education sufficient to enable me to qualify for work in the government service undertaken in the main only by university graduates.

While I went one way, my chum George Prodgers went on to become a professional hockey player. The newspapers gave him the name of "Goldie" and as "Goldie" Prodgers he became a star who played for several great teams. Playing for the Montreal Canadiens in a Stanley Cup final he took a pass from the famous Newsey Lalonde and scored the goal which won the championship for the Canadiens. Later he managed several professional and semi-professional clubs. He died in 1935.

I do not want to leave the impression that a boy's life in London in the 1890's was all work, school and rebellion against both. Far from it. On the whole I liked carrying papers and the friends I made doing so and the rewards it brought. I may not have liked school, but many children did. I belonged to the Sunday School of the Cronyn Memorial Church which was Anglican, and I used to enjoy immensely reading the books of G.A.Henty which were in the Sunday School library. I also belonged to the Boys Brigade at the Church, and went to picnics and weekend camps at Port Stanley and at Springbank Park down the river from London. What I really remember and still feel a pleasure in remembering is the freedom and happiness which boys felt in the spring in those days in Ontario now long gone.

In his books about Tom Sawyer and Huckleberry Finn, Mark Twain succeeded in putting into words what it felt like to be a boy in a town or small city, distant from the frontier, the settlers and the Indians but still close to the country, and the birds, the animals and the forest. And what Mark Twain wrote about is the truth. For example, most parents in London used to forbid their children to go barefoot—at least to school —on account of the danger of cuts, injuries and infections, but more because bare feet were not respectable. The prohibition on bare feet did not work very well, particularly in the summer holidays. After the passing of three quarters of a century I can still remember vividly the pleasure and excitement and joy I used to experience when I got my boots and stockings off, and could feel the warm, grey dust of the roads of London between my toes, and the fresh tingle of the cold dew on the grass in the morning and the sweet warmth of the board sidewalks and the tiny prickle of the splinters which passed away once one's feet were hard and calloused.

And there was the "old swimming hole". Most parents forbade their boys (girls were not expected to swim except under close supervision and in swimming costumes at places like Port Stanley) to swim in the Thames River which flowed through London. The reasons for this prohibition were similar to those applied to barefeet; danger and want of respectability. Swimming in the buff, as we called it, was not decent. But the prohibition did not work. Swimming in "Swiftwater" was a regular sport for all but the worst sissies. From William Street, where my home was, we used to walk "up to the valley", where the campus of the University of Western Ontario now is. Here in the north fork of the Thames was a still, deep pool below a small rapid where the water flowing over hard rocks for ages had made a hole in the earth and softer rocks. I suppose it was dangerous, but I never recall anyone drowning or being hurt in the Swiftwater, although I do remember quite well how on one occasion we had to fish George Prodgers out of the pool and empty the water out of him. What a pleasure to throw off one's clothes and dive or belly-flop into the cool waters, and swim about and splash each other in the face! In July and August the temperature in that part of the peninsula of western Ontario rises frequently above ninety degrees Fahrenheit, and the humidity, good for crops, is terrible for people and animals. All the greater, therefore, was the cool freshness of an "old swimming hole" at the Swiftwater and further away at the Bend where one could swim further and lark about among the trees. Somehow swimming and chasing about naked on the river bank and among the trees made one feel strong and fresh and free. It was a wonderful feeling, and one forgot completely that one's parents were going to look askance at one's wet hair and say, "Where have you been?" and the reply was going to be "Aw, it was so hot I stuck my head in the rain barrel." And the comment was going to follow: "I bet! Come and get your supper!" Sometimes I got a clip on the ear, but no serious effort was ever made to save me from the sin and danger of swimming in the Swiftwater.

Then there was Brown's Bush. This was a small remainder of the ancient forest of western Ontario which was not far from my home. Because of the nature of the terrain, a small hill running down to a swamp which was usually dry in summer, Brown's Bush had never been divided up and sold as building land, nor had it even been used except as a place where the owner's cattle pastured and sheltered from the summer sun. Many trees of a great age and size remained in Brown's Bush; beech, maples, oak, hickory and chestnut, not to mention bush chestnuts which produced sweet, edible nuts. Here we children could escape from the sun into cool, mossy shade, and we let our imaginations run free recreating the past as we had learned about it second and third hand in stories and tales about Indians and animals and soldiers. We hunted each other in games like hide and seek and run sheep run, and we lounged about in gangs and bands, some real and most imaginary. For us the days of violence when the Donnelly Boys killed and were killed in the back concessions near London were not long past. Our mothers used to sing to the children a variation of the ditty of the Scottish border about the Black Douglas

> "Hush ye, Hush, little Pet ye
> Or the Donnelly Boys'll come and get ye."

And we could sometimes imagine that among the trees of Brown's Bush the Donnelly Boys were still at large. This filled us with delicious fear and horror.

In the 1890's there could still be found in London many of the natural features of the land. I have mentioned the small water course which my grandfather Dickens found on his land when the spring broke in 1872. This flowed into Carling's Creek which disappeared many years ago into a large sewer and can be seen no more. Carling's Creek was crossed in my young days by foot bridges at many points, and in the spring or at moments of heavy rainfall these bridges were often awash with the swollen waters of what became for a few days at a time a deep river with a strong current. Here I had my first adventure —one of the several close calls which I have had in my lifetime. I was too young, however, to remember it, and it has come down to me from my family how my sister was out walking me in my "baby buggy" and how, her attention being diverted, the buggy rolled down the slope of the bank of Carling's Creek. When my sister turned around I was floating away. She let out a great shriek. A cobbler named John Guymer rushed out of his shop, ran along the bank, waded into the water and, thus, I am able to remember the incident.

Carling's Creek ran through the flat land below Carling's heights, a low elevation of land near my home where there was located Wolsley Barracks, and the parade ground and field for manoeuvres of the small garrison of the Canadian regular forces. Ordinarily there was not great activity about the Barracks, but in the summer months Carling's Heights became a great centre of activity and excitement when the militia formations from all over the military district of which London was the centre assembled for their summer camp and for their training. In those days soldiers wore splendid colored uniforms of red and green and blue, and gold braid flashed about and white pipe clay shone. The cavalry regiments and the Light Horse Artillery were exciting to watch. Every Sunday the regiments assembled shined up and smart for a Church Parade. I remember particularly one of the smartest infantry companies, the 28th Foot from Berlin, Ontario. These militia men used to sing a very melodious and catchy song a few words of which still stick in my mind.

The Deutsch Company
Is the best Company
Which ever came over

From old Germany."

In the evenings we used to see little groups of militia men trooping off down town singing and chattering and shouting on their way to the bars, shops and hotels off Dundas Street in the centre of London.

Militia camp or no militia camp there was every evening a ceremonial at the barracks which always fascinated us, even though it happened so often that it was as much a part of daily life as washing before breakfast. This was the sounding of the last post. The bugler was a Canadian regular soldier, Tom Walsh, who lived on William Street. He sounded notes which were pure and true, and they floated across the houses from Carling's Heights in a clear, beautiful way. I often wondered whether or not this was the reason my Ferns grandparents lived on William Street, because they always became silent and listened for Tom Walsh's bugle sounding in a way which they had known for so many years in India. Sometimes we used to watch the soldiers hauling down the Union Jack, with its rich colors: real red, real blue and real white.

When I reflect upon the important matters of religion and politics and what I learned about both when I was a boy, I am bound to say that I cannot recall much about these subjects. Delivering a Tory newspaper was a matter of business not an act of faith or support. In a vague way we were all Tories. By "we" I mean all the Protestants, who were the majority. I was taken to Church and to Sunday School. My mother was a regular attender at the Cronyn Memorial Church, and she always subscribed to the *Christian Herald*, which she read and encouraged her children to read. In spite of this exposure to the Christian religion from my infancy I cannot say that I learned anything specific about it which sticks in my conscious mind. I found the stories from the Bible boring and tiresome, and their larger meaning was lost on me. On the other hand I did learn about right and wrong, and I learned to pray. Whenever I have been in a jam or tight place, and this has occurred often enough in my life, I pray, and more often than not my prayers have been answered. I never pray for things like money or success, but when I am up against it I pray for a break which will enable me to survive. Prayer, I found, affects one's conduct. I am naturally hell-bent, and my natural inclination has always been towards committing, if not all, at least a majority of the seven deadly sins which destroy oneself and others. But gratitude to God has always held me back, and I think I can say that, although I have often been foolish, I have never been wicked. If this is so I think I learned about the management of myself from the church in London and from the example of those who belonged to it.

To me faith is the substance of things hoped for; the evidence of things unseen. That is why talk about religion has never very much interested or influenced me. Much of it bored me because it was so often concerned with matters which are only of temporary importance. This is illustrated, I think, by the fact that my only memory of specific teaching in Church concerns the confirmation class I attended. We discussed problems of youth, and the problem we discussed which I remember was our use of slang—not the secret rude language which did sometimes trouble my conscience—but the use of phrases such as "Cut it out". One youngster asked the curate who was teaching us, the Rev. Arthur Carlyle, later a bishop, what you could say instead of "Cut it out", and he replied, "You might say, 'Please omit it'."

If I learned something about faith in my home and church, I learned bigotry in the town. This, I think, I have pretty thoroughly lost through travelling about Canada and knocking around with all kinds of people. Practically everyone among our class of people was influenced by the bigotry brought to Ontario from Ireland. The 17 March, St. Patrick's Day, and the 12 July, Orangeman's Day, always brought on tension. We children used to chant rhymes aimed at the Catholics. One of them, I remember, went like this

"Teeter, Totter, Holy Water
Sprinkle the Catholics everywhere

29

And if that won't do
We'll cut them in two
And bury them under the Orange and Blue.

Catholics married Protestants, of course, but this almost seemed unnatural and was always a matter of anxiety, tension and adverse comment. Turning Catholic, or vice-versa, indicated feeble-mindedness or wisdom, depending on one's religious persuasion. In spite of this sort of feeling people worked together and the tensions of St. Patricks's Day and Orangeman's Day never resulted in more than a few bruises from shillelaghs. But the feelings were real enough.

As to feelings about other matters I cannot remember much. The Irish were hot about being Irish, but the English were different. Although my parents and grandparents were English by birth we did not seem to have as much patriotism or feeling about England as the Irish had about Ireland. There was an Englishmen's Picnic, and Englishmen helped each other, but this was more a matter of where one came from in the "old country" than of coming from England. There were common catches illustrative of this such as

I be Devon
What be ye?
I be Devon tae.
or   By Tre, Pol, and Pen
You know the Cornishmen.

Native born children of English parents like myself lost this sort of identity with England. We developed the common contempt felt for English immigrants which expressed itself in sneers about "green English men" and "Sparrows".

Immigrants from the British Isles were, of course, only additions to the solid core of London citizenry. These were for the most part Ontarians who had lived for two, three or four generations in Ontario, and had developed their own character and way of life. There was a constant influx into London of families from rural Ontario. It was said that London was the place where good farmers go to die. It certainly was a town

30

where farmers, once they had "made it", bought property, made investments and built substantial homes for their old age. They, too, had their loyalties to one another. There were many stories illustrative of the clannishness of the people from the rural counties of Ontario. The men from Bruce County were particularly noted for this quality, and many of them had settled in London after a lifetime of shipping produce to the market in London. One story about them concerned a magistrate in London who came from Bruce County. It was observed that those up before this magistrate who, when asked their name and place of residence, replied, "So and so, Bruce County," were always dealt with more leniently than offenders from other parts of Ontario or the world. One day a Chinese laundryman was summoned to appear on a charge of doing business on Sunday. He was asked the question about name and place of residence and he promptly replied, "Me from Bloose, too."

In London in the 1890's there were very few people whose mother tongue was not English. It was a matter for remark when a Greek opened the Olympia Restaurant sometime about 1905. There were a few Chinese who ran hand laundries. There were very few Jews. Levi Fox, who ran a jeweller's shop, was regarded as an exceptionable being not on account of his business or his appearance or his habits, but on account of his religion. It was said that Jews could not flourish in London because of the number of Scots Ontarians.

There were a few blacks in London. One family, the Martins, lived on Miles Street which backs immediately on William Street. The three Martin boys went to St. George's School, and my sisters and I often played with them and were in and out of their home. Their grandfather was a contemporary of my grandparents. He had been a slave in the United States, and had fled to freedom under the British Crown in Canada. Two of the Martin boys became sleeping car porters on one of the railways, and the third, who was "good at school", migrated to the United States, where he became a high executive in the

Young Men's Christian Association in North Carolina.

Another notable character was Bec Logan, a black woman who lived in a shanty near the corner of Miles Street on Pall Mall. She was a large woman who always wore a leather belt around her middle. In her young days she had been the mistress of the playboy brother of a prominent citizen of London, and she had had a daughter by him. He had established her in her home, and she worked in the Wolsley Barracks. She had social pretensions. One day her daughter, Susan, was playing with some of the children roundabout. She came out and shouted: "Hey, you Sal, come in here and stop playin' with them white trash. Don't you know your uncle's a Member of Parliament." Sal went to Detroit, and sent home two of her children to be raised by her mother.

As to being British this was not stongly felt. Of course there was some satisfaction in knowing one was part of something large and important in the world. This was especially so in the presence of Americans who were great braggarts on account of the size, growth, beauty, democratic character etc. of the United States. A lot of American bragging and self confident enthusiasm about their country rubbed off on us. No one thought twice about going to "make good" in the United States. New York was regarded as a unique and wonderful city. All this existed alongside a vague feeling of dislike for the United States and a feeling of moral superiority to a country where "anything goes". We regarded Canada as a more law abiding and decent country, poorer certainly but better.

As children in London I think we all had some sense of the dangers and perils to life caused by disease, "bad times" and by the fallibility of individuals and oneself. As in the matter of going barefoot or swimming in the Swiftwater, this sense that life was a perilous and uncertain proposition never much deterred us from enjoying ourselves. We all had to work hard to survive, but this was enjoyable. I have never understood what pleasure can be derived from having no work to do. Disease carried off many children, but we took this as a matter of course. Three of my wife's sisters died in childhood. Our family was rather unusual in that all six children born of my mother grew up and lived to old age. Only two of five of my Grandmother Ferns' children survived to old age, and only three out of six of my Grandmother Dickens did so. In the matter of survival there had probably been some progress. I know that I would have died with diphtheria had it not been for a doctor who, when I was choking to death, stuck a tube down my throat which enabled me to breathe long enough to survive. Before I had diphtheria, I was a rather good boy soprano. After diphtheria I was no longer so, and I like to think that diphtheria robbed me of a career as an opera singer, which was always a secret ambition of mine.

3

From every point of view—even the most short-term—my decision to leave school before my thirteenth birthday was a mistake. As a paper boy I had been earning $2.00—$2.50 a week, and I was going to school and enjoying myself in the holidays. As a working man going on thirteen I found myself employed for approximately 60 hours a week at $2.50, and I provided my own capital equipment—my bicycle.

My new condition of "independence" had a glamour which blinded me to my foolishness. I was now grown-up, or so I thought. When I think about it now, I was probably having a similar experience to the young fools nowadays who get married or run off with girls at the age of 15 or 16. Unrestrained by my parents, who had, or should have had, more experience of life and its necessities, I had made what seemed to me a glorious step forward. I had become a man: five to ten years too soon, as it turned out.

My first job, however, plunged me into a new and exciting life in the centre of London. I was employed as a delivery boy and general factotum in Ashplant's Shoe Store at the corner of Market Lane and Dundas Street. The proprietor, Mr. Hubert Ashplant, was a Devonshire man who had retained his thick Devonshire accent. He watched the pennies as carefully as any Scots Ontarian, but he was a jovial pleasant man whom I liked very much. When I decided to quit my job and "go west" he said, "Stay with me, Bub, and I'll make a man of you. And I'll give you another two bits a week." (25 cents)

34

Before this happened, I had a few splendid months amid the rush and bustle of Covent Garden Market in London. This was a large handsome structure, which has now been torn down and replaced by a multi-storey car park. It occupied a whole city block between the rear of the shops on Dundas Street and King Street in one direction and in the other direction between the rear of the shops and houses on Talbot Street and the rear of the shops and offices on Richmond Street. The great market hall stood in the middle of the square with arcades along two sides. Here the farmers from twenty miles around London brought their produce—butter, eggs, bacon, sausages, meat, milk, honey, maple syrup, green vegetables, fruit, poultry and game—for sale directly to the consumers. Goods were displayed in stalls under cover, or on the backs of wagons in the open or under the arcades. The clerk of the market allocated space and collected the market fee each day. The farmers backed their wagons into place, unhitched their horses, and took them to the stables behind the hotels on King Street. Their wives or children set out the produce for sale, and the market day got under way. There were very few families in London who did not buy some or all of their provisions at Covent Garden Market, and much else besides. People always seemed to swarm there, especially on Saturdays, or in the fruit season which started with the strawberries in May and did not end until the last hard apples were picked in September.

This way of doing business was the secret of London's growth and eventually of its great wealth. The profits made elsewhere by middlemen went directly into the farmer's pockets, and the consumer benefited from the competition of the farmers. The farmers invested money in London: in property, in insurance and trusts and in industry. It is in no way surprising that a Mayor of London, Sir Adam Beck, was the man who led the fight to supply electrical power to consumers of all kinds directly without middlemen in the shape of "investors" levying a toll on the supply of energy generated

35

from the rivers of Ontario. Nobody ever made a "killing" out of the Ontario Hydro, and the most an investor could get was the fixed interest on a bond or debenture. The result was that industry, farmers and private householders got the cheapest energy in the world, and thus became productive and prosperous. In my view this developed out of the way of doing business which grew up in the Covent Garden Market in London.

There was more to the market than buying and selling. On Saturday evenings the medicine men, jugglers, musicians, witch doctors, preachers, magicians and con men made their pitch in the light of flares and torches. People were urged to buy patent medicine "to cure the gout, pains within and pains without". You could try to out-smart the magicians and con men. You could listen to music. Strong farm boys could measure their strength against professional strong men who could bend iron bars or wield mighty hammers. In the bars and hotels along King Street, men could get drunk or "get put". The ultimate in sin and dissipation was the Bucket of Blood on the corner of York and Rideout Street. One could find salvation or damnation in the Covent Garden Market and its adjacent community, but being London and being Ontario most people sought more of one than the other.

One lesson you had to learn was not to believe everything people said. On my first day in Ashplant's Shoe Store a clerk in the store instructed me, for example, to go out and buy some white lamp black. He told me where to go and what to ask for, and I fell for it.

Apart from delivering parcels and fetching and carrying around the shop, one of my tasks was practical advertising. One of Mr. Ashplant's specialties was copper toed, heavy leather farm boots. Boys' sizes sold for 90 cents a pair and men's for $1.10. Mr. Ashplant believed, and I think he was right, that these boots needed to be made attractive and noticeable to customers. This was obvious because there was nothing about them which could bring anyone much delight. They were strictly for duty. To correct the impression created by

36

these clodhoppers, Mr. Ashplant set me the task of polishing the copper toes of each boot until they shone brightly. This was a pretty continuous job because the copper soon discoloured with verdigris. I used to burnish the copper until it glowed. Then I tied the laces of the boots together and hung the boots on one of the many hooks fastened in a pole. When I had done 12 or 15 pairs in this way, I lifted the pole up and hooked it onto a ring outside the front door of the shop. There was a sort of tree of boots each glistening and bright. On a sunny day it was a pretty sight, and I think this helped Mr. Ashplant to sell farm boots simply because they had a momentary charm like a wrapping on a modern candy bar or a package of cigarettes.

In spite of the glamour and excitement of working in and around Covent Garden Market, I did not stay long with Ashplant's Shoe Store. The call of the wild was too strong. Like Huckleberry Finn I was resolved to light out for the territories. Not the Northwest Territories, but the next best thing: Algoma, an area of Ontario north of Lake Superior of which there were then great expectations. A steel plant was being planned at Sault Sainte Marie, and as always happens in Canada people began to talk about the Soo being as big as Chicago in so many years time. Although I was only approaching my thirteenth birthday, I must have caught the fever for I was strongly minded to quit London. Leaving London was not so adult or so bold as it sounds, because I had an opportunity to go to Algoma to my uncle, Joe Dickens and his family.

Joe Dickens was a restless man. Never endowed greatly with material goods, he nonetheless had good luck; a good luck which on several occasions enabled him to live when others around him perished. One instance of this occurred in 1881 when he was only thirteen years old. He was a passenger on the S.S. Victoria, a paddle wheel pleasure steamer which carried people from London to Springbank Park a few miles down the Thames. On the day when Joe Dickens was a passenger too many people crowded to one side of the vessel: she

37

turned turtle trapping most of the passengers in the water. Over 200 people perished, but Joe Dickens was not one of them. He was below decks looking at the engine of the boat when she turned over. Thus he was able to escape, and was one of few dragged ashore. He arrived home on foot wet and scratched and was put to bed with "brain fever".

He was not more than sixteen when he enlisted in the 7th Fusiliers, a London militia regiment, in order to help put down the second rebellion in the Northwest Territories headed by Louis Riel. The railway carried the 7th Fusiliers as far as Swift Current, in what is now the province of Saskatchewan. This was the closest point to the South Saskatchewan River down which the regiment was to be transported by boats to the scene of the fighting. The South Saskatchewan is a lazy river, but a capricious one. Weather changes several hundred miles away in the mountains affect its water levels, often suddenly. Joe and his fellow soldiers camped by the South Saskatchewan. During the night the water rose several feet in a few hours. The encampment was inundated; the supplies of food were ruined, and word came that the war was over.

When my uncle Joe returned from the Northwest Territories he settled down and served an apprenticeship in the metal working trade. He was a core maker, which is a skilled job connected with metal casting. He specialized in brass. After ten years or so of metal casting and marriage Joe listened to the tales of his wife's family, the Lefflers who had gone from London to homestead in Algoma. It was my uncle Joe's place to which I decided to go in June 1901.

I was in Algoma from then until March, 1903. Already Joe Dickens had discovered that one could not build a productive farm of the kind which existed around London, Ontario, among the rocks of Algoma. He was making a bare living off his holding of 160 acres by cutting the only real crop on his homestead: the pulpwood forest. My job was "doing the chores", and cutting the wood for heating the district school, a contract for the supply of which my Uncle Joe had. Sometimes there was not much of anything to do and I developed a taste for reading. Unfortunately the only reading matter available was the *Family Herald,* a fat journal published in Montreal which contained more advertising than intellectual nourishment. My Aunt Connie's taste in literature was strongly inclined to the lightest of romantic stories which, after I read two or three, became extremely boring. I think that, had I had access to a good encyclopaedia at that time, I would have benefited greatly.

As it was I went to work for a man named Lemon swamping cedar logs. Swamping logs was a term used for the process of dragging logs from the point in the forest where the trees had been cut down, trimmed and cut into the required lengths, to the point on the shore of Lake Superior where they were piled awaiting the moment when they would be floated on the water, formed into a great boom, and towed to the lumber mills. My job was to drive a single horse harnessed to a wiffle tree which in turn was fastened to a heavy chain. This chain was then fixed to the log in a kind of loop knot. Walking by the log with the reins in one's hands, one guided the horse through the forest and among the stumps, releasing the log skidding along the surface from any obstruction it might encounter. There was some danger of breaking either an arm or a leg, but I was fortunate and managed to survive the job. I liked the forest, and soon I was able to find my way about in a fashion which mystified and amazed newcomers, who saw in the forest just a lot of trees haphazardly placed there to confuse them and hide landmarks for their guidance.

I had acquired a .22 calibre rifle and I played at being a hunter. I never saw game bigger than partridge and rabbits. By 1902 all the big animals like deer and moose had been killed or had fled elsewhere, and yet sixty years later, when I went to look at the Dickens homestead, I saw moose roaming free in the woods within sight of the road allowance. Besides partridge and rabbits there were girls at large in the woods in 1902 hunting for the satyrs of Algoma. I remember particularly the Leffler girls who were the cousins of my cousins. What later happened to them I do not know, but their brother Lyle made a curious and successful career for himself. He became a medicine man, with a large establishment near Rockwood, Ontario. Most farmers raise alfalfa as a fodder crop, but Lyle grew it for human consumption. He was a master advertiser who persuaded the public that alfalfa tea is a health giving remedy for a variety of ailments, and on the strength of faith in alfalfa Lyle made himself a very good living.

I learned about life in Algoma, and I encountered the nearness of death. One evening after work my cousin, a French-Canadian boy and I were fooling around in a punt on Goulais Bay. This is a broad expanse of water opening into Lake Superior, and this evening it was as quiet as a mill pond. We had one good oar and one broken, and the punt was leaky. None the less we ventured about a mile out into the bay. As the sun went down the wind began to blow off shore driving us towards the open Lake. In storm Lake Superior is as savage as the North Atlantic, and we were soon being driven towards it and certain death. As the night fell we were toiling with our poor oars, and the waves and darkness seemed to spell the end of us. This was one of the times I prayed. But I kept bailing and paddling with the broken oar. My Uncle Joe and the others on shore lit a huge bonfire, and this gave us a point to aim at if only we could prevail against the wind, and keep the punt from sinking. After some hours we managed to make the shore where the bonfire blazed. My fear of boating is still with me, and I do not like even a vessel of 25,000 tons.

By the spring of 1903 Uncle Joe had had enough of Algoma. Leaving his wife and three boys—Charlie, Harvey and Lloyd—behind at the homestead, he and I returned to London. Joe found a job as a metal mechanic and core maker in the railway workshops at Stratford, Ontario. He lived there for the rest of his life until he died at the age of eighty-nine in 1957. He had one more irresistible fit of restlessness in his life, however. By falsifying his age he was able to enlist in the 18th Battalion of the City of London Regiment and he went overseas in 1915. In the trenches in France he encountered another instance of extraordinary luck in the matter of survival. One night he and another soldier were patrolling in a trench near St. Eloi. This consisted of Joe walking a certain distance in the trench, turning around and walking back to the point where he met the soldier who was patrolling in the opposite direction. About 2 a.m. he and the other soldier met, exchanged a few words amid the racket of the bombardment and turned on their separate marches along the trench. A star shell exploded overhead and Joe looked back at his companion. He was nowhere to be seen. He could not have run away, for there was no place for him to run to. He was never found, nor any part of him.

Joe was luckier than his eldest son. Charlie enlisted in the Mounted Infantry. He never felt a horse beneath him, but he had a lot to do with telephone equipment. One night he and six others were in a forward post giving the position of gun flashes from the German Artillery. When others came to relieve them in the morning they were all found dead, not a mark on them, killed apparently by the shock wave of a high explosive.

In March, 1903, I arrived back home. I soon found a job as a delivery boy with a firm of family grocers and butchers located at the corner of Maitland Street and Central Avenue: Cohoon and Patterson. The two partners had married each other's sister, and so this business was very much a family affair. Mr. Patterson and his wife lived over the shop and Mr. and Mrs. Cohoon lived a short distance away in a large dwelling with a considerable carriage shed. I became one of the family, for I ate my meals with them, and was busy with the tasks they set me from early morning until late at night. No matter how late it was I never failed to rub down the firm's delivery horses. Every Saturday night I gave them their special treat: a hot bran mash. I think that my days with Cohoon and

41

Patterson were the happiest in all my life.

A grocery and butcher business in the early years of this century was much different from what we see today. Grocers and butchers were not merely distributors of packages of this and that. Canned and packaged goods sold under brand names there were, of course, but much of what was sold to customers was bought in barrels, sacks and boxes, and the grocer weighed and packaged what the customers ordered often under the customer's own eyes. One of our jobs of Friday night was to make up twenty pound bags of sugar in readiness for Saturday's trade. These sold at a special price: $1.00. As butchers Cohoon and Patterson did not kill their own animals, but all meat was delivered to them in carcases, which they cut up according to the customers' requirements. A grocery store was not a spacious, air conditioned, sanitized arrangement of shelves and refrigerators. It was a crowded cave full of the most delicious odours, and busy with the activity of clerks wrapping and bagging goods, gossiping and joking with customers who were not infrequently sampling the firm's prunes in an open barrel or the hard candy in a waxed wooden pail. The flavour of the cheese was demonstrated to the customers by offering them a small slice, and I can remember on one occasion Mr. Patterson popping upstairs to get a slice of bacon his wife was frying in order to provide a sample of his produce for a customer. The retail grocer was an expert in buying produce from farmers, manufacturers and wholesalers. He was also a species of banker inasmuch as most customers ran accounts, and some were so slow paying that Cohoon and Patterson were a kind of domestic finance company. My services were esteemed because, being young and impudent, I developed the ability to sweet-talk some of the housewives into paying up when I delivered their orders. Once I carried this too far and the lady of the house chased me out with a broom just at the moment when Mr. and Mrs. Cohoon were passing in their carriage, out for their regular Wednesday afternoon drive into the country. The import of what I had been up to was the subject of much ragging and joking, but Mr. Patterson simply said, "It's all right, Bub, Mrs. McKay has always been poor pay, and always will be." But Cohoon and Patterson went on supplying her with groceries and meat as long as I worked for them.

Both partners and their wives were extremely hard working people. No matter how late or hard they worked Saturday night and on into the early hours of the next morning they were always up early Sunday, bathed, brushed and clothed in their best and off on foot to the Presbyterian Church. They were of Ulster descent, but there was nothing of bigotry in them. They were among the jolliest, nicest people I ever knew. Martha Cohoon had lived in New York before her marriage, and she infected me with wonder about that great city, the magic place of the Americas.

Just why I did not stay in the grocery trade I do not know. Above all else I wanted to work out of doors, and I wanted to earn "big money". One of the obvious outdoor employments was bricklaying. By 1880 or thereabouts lumber as a building material for whole houses was becoming relatively expensive, and ideas of solidity and elegance were changing. London was becoming much more a brick built city in the late 1880's and in the 1890's building in brick, sometimes with stone trim, was very general. Factories, churches and schools as well as private homes were all of brick. There were opportunities in the building business. Furthermore bricklayers and stone masons were well-paid craftsmen. A journeyman bricklayer could make as much as $30.00 a week.

In a way I had a family connection with the building trade. My mother's sister, Aunt Lily, had married the eldest son of John Hayman, a bricklayer and stonemason who had come from Devonshire many years previously. John Hayman was a building contractor of some importance in London, and was on the way towards the wealth which enabled some of his descendants to ride to hounds with the London Hunt. He was a strong, hard and hard working man. He had several sons, and all of them worked for their father. And they worked. Old

43

John Hayman was a hard driver, and he was known to have taken a knotted rope to any of his boys, even when grown men, who did not apply themselves diligently to the task in hand.

I was apprenticed to the firm of Hayman and Sons early in 1905. By this time John Hayman's eldest son, my uncle by marriage, was dead. He had fallen down the shaft of a hoist, landed on his head on a barrow loaded with bricks, and so ended his life leaving behind a widow and a small son, my cousin, Harold Hayman. Thus, when I started with the Hayman's the family connection was not very immediate and real.

I only lasted a few months with them. Hard as it was carrying hods of bricks and working on the "sweat board" mixing with a shovel, I did not mind this so much as the "riding" I had to endure at the hands of the Hayman boys. "The Hayman Boys" is how they were spoken of on account of the very real presence of the patriarch John Hayman, but they were in fact all grown men, ten or more years older than I was. Willy, the youngest, I particularly hated on account of the nasty way he sneered at my ignorance of the trade and my natural innocence. Most apprentices had to put up with a good deal of kidding at their expense, but there was more to Willy's nastiness than joking about a greenhorn.

One day I was working with a "green Englishman" in the basement of a building. We were laying a cement floor, and seemingly working alone together. I did not notice Willy Hayman at work on a scaffold just out of our line of vision. This was unfortunate because I began to give tongue to my views of the Haymans and Willy in particular. I expanded upon what I was going to do if I was not taken off cement work and given an opportunity to "work on the line", i.e. to start laying bricks. The next day I was fired.

I never troubled to discover whether my articles of indenture provided for instant dismissal. Within twenty-four hours I had packed my telescope, a collapsible canvas bag, and I was on my way to "the West" to work in the harvest fields. I had enough for the fare to Winnipeg: $17.00. I could return for an additional $5.00 provided I stayed in "the West" for three months. Equally as important, a letter of introduction was sent from the Cohoon family to one of their kinsmen, Tom Bere, who farmed at Mather, Manitoba. On the train to Toronto, where one section of the harvest special was made up, I fell in with a farmer from near London, Uriah MacRoberts, who used to supply butter to my parents. He was on his way west to hunt for land, and he had a well stocked hamper of bread, cheese and roasted chickens to which I was able to add a stock of sandwiches and apples. He had the additional advantage, I was to discover, of being large, strong, sober and sensible.

The same cannot be said of the assortment of miners, labourers and immigrants who boarded the Special in the Toronto station. There were no women among the passengers and just as well. The miners, the most numerous group, and a good many of the rest had provisioned themselves for the journey lasting from Tuesday night to Friday morning with ample supplies of whiskey. By the time the train had cleared the Toronto yards on the way to North Bay most of the passengers were drunk. By the middle of the night the floors and seats were soaked in vomit, and the drunks lay three deep in the aisles, so that the conductor and the trainmen were obliged to walk on the arms of the seats while they punched the tickets after each of the divisional stops. It was an eerie and disgusting scene; the dimly lit swaying coach and the train crew clamouring above the sprawled out inebriates, the trainman holding his lantern while the conductor looked at the tickets he had with difficulty obtained from the drunken and often ill-tempered holders.

The train running over the Grand Trunk tracks to North Bay joined the Canadian Pacific train from Montreal to make up the complete Harvest Special. The Special was only special in name. It had the lowest priority of anything moving on the line, which meant that it had to "take the hole" giving preference on sidings even to cattle and freight trains moving east and west on the single track which at that time spanned Canada from Montreal to Vancouver. Hence the time it took to travel from Toronto to Winnipeg; three nights and two days.

On Wednesday morning hunger followed on thirst, and the men who had provided themselves with whiskey and not food had no means of eating. About every 140—150 miles along the transcontinental railway there were divisional points where the train stopped for twenty minutes or half an hour to take on fuel and water and where the train crew checked over the running equipment and the locomotive. At the divisional points there were settlements of varying size and a few shops and often a lunch counter in the station which sold a few items of food. When a hoard of hungry men descended on a divisional point this resembled an attack by barbarians. Some did not have time to pay for what they took, and many had no intention of doing so. They raided gardens to pull up carrots and anything edible. Word went ahead of the train by telegraph. At the succeeding divisional points people were ready armed with stones, pitchforks and even shot guns.

At Nipigon, Ontario, there was a great fight among the passengers. It came about in this way. The coaches on the train were colonist cars which meant that these cars had bunks in them above the seats so that passengers could sleep stretched out, and not sprawled on wooden slatted seats as they were in the ordinary "day coaches" which made up a part of ordinary trains. By day men sat on the edge of the bunks swinging their legs in the aisle. Once or twice miners passing through the colonist cars had been hit by the swinging legs of the labourers, who could not speak English. A few times miners so offended had thrown punches at "the hunkies" and the "hunkies" had replied by smashing the miners on their heads with beer bottles. By the time we reached Nipigon blood was up, and the miners and the foreign born poured out of the train and set to in the station yard. Nobody could stop the battle. It ended only when the engineer blew the whistle and set the train in motion. There was a great outcry, and men bleeding and torn raced after the train and scrambled aboard. Fortunately for them the Harvest Special did not accelerate very rapidly. Later, I am told, North-West Mounted Police constables rode the Harvest Specials. For my part I either kept close to Uriah MacRoberts or rode on the platform between the cars.

We arrived in Winnipeg on Friday morning. The train to Deloraine, Manitoba, towards which I was heading, had already left when the Harvest Special pulled into the station. Uriah MacRoberts and I put up at the Sutherland Hotel on Main Street north of the C.P.R. tracks. I had a chance to look around downtown Winnipeg. At that time the Winnipeg station of the C.P.R. was just under construction in brick and marble, and the Royal Alexandra Hotel, which set a standard of magnificence in Winnipeg for half a century, was just being started. There was then no subway to carry Main Street under the C.P.R. tracks. Main Street and Portage Avenue seemed enormous, and so they were in comparison with the narrow main streets of Ontario towns. They were paved with cedar blocks, and electric tram cars ran down the centres of the great thoroughfares. There was only one tall building on Main Street then; the Union Bank on the corner of William Avenue. It rose ten storeys or more above the street. The other buildings were all one, two, three and at the most four storeys. On Portage Avenue the T. Eaton Company had just turned the first sod of their enormous department store, but one could not yet judge its size. The famous Hudson's Bay Company had a large store and headquarters on Main Street south of Portage Avenue near the junction of the Red and Assiniboine Rivers. There was an air of expectancy and energy about Winnipeg, and I could feel it.

The next morning I took the train which went west, but south of the main line of the C.P.R. At La Riviere I had some lunch. I still remember the pleasure and surprise at the lovely

47

trees which could be seen in this part of Manitoba as the train pulled slowly up the valley. Pilot Mound, a great artificial hill built by a forgotten people some time in the remote past, was both startling and impressive. About four in the afternoon I reached Mather, Manitoba, where I was met by Fairy Bere, one of the four children of Tom Bere.

I spent ten days stooking on the Bere Place. What is stooking? The word like the job it describes is dead and gone, and yet stooking was until World War II a muscle aching piece of essential hand work in the partially mechanised harvesting of the 100. 200, 300, 400 million bushels of grain which grew on the prairies of Western Canada.

To understand stooking it is necessary to describe the process of harvesting as it was in the West half a century and more ago. The crops grew in the great square fields which had been ploughed by horses or oxen, harrowed and disced by horse-drawn machines and planted by horse-drawn seeders. Horses and men were the almost universal source of power on the farms except for the process of threshing. In those days animals were more reliable than steam tractors or the new fangled gasoline driven tractors. Above all they worked on a fuel which the farmer grew himself on his own place. Horses provided the energy for a number of machines of which the most intricate and impressive was the binder. This was a machine which cut the grain standing in uniform rows in the fields. As the moving blade of the binder cut the standing grain about four or five inches from its roots the stalks fell on moving canvas belt which conveyed it to a mechanism which gathered the stalks of grain into a sheaf and then bound it with a piece of twine which the very ingenious knotting device tied. Once this was accomplished the sheaf was then deposited on the stubble as the binder moved forward at a rate of about four to six miles an hour. The energy for all this cutting, gathering, binding and knotting was generated by two or more horses drawing the binder forward and causing a broad iron wheel with cleats on its surface to turn, bearing part of the

48

weight of the machine and at the same time delivering the energy to the mechanism by a system of cogs and gears. The binder most commonly used on the prairies was made by a Canadian firm, the Massey-Harris Company, but there were also binders made by the John Deere Plough Company and others.

The binder left the sheaves on the stubble. What is a sheaf? Sheaves of grain are on the coat of arms of the province of Saskatchewan. A sheaf of grain is today as archaic an object as a battle axe on the arms of an English Earl, and its purpose less well understood. A sheaf was a bundle of stalks of grain. The bundle differed in weight depending on what cereal grain was in the bundle, how good the crop was and how dry the stalks were. A sheaf of oats in a poor year might weigh only five pounds, and a sheaf of wheat in a good year harvesting forty bushels to the acre, as much as twenty pounds or more.

Stooking was the task of gathering the sheafs and setting them on end, the heads of the grain uppermost, in stooks, or little stacks of sheaves. The purpose of the exercise was to get the heads off the ground to avoid damp and to allow for further drying. Generally eight to twelve sheaves made a stook. Sometimes one or two sheaves were placed on the top of the stook if the weather was not good, and threatened rain or snow. Yes, I have seen snow during the harvest in Alberta. Stooking from seven in the morning until nightfall with a break for lunch and a pause for a drink of tea or water about four p.m. is hard work.

The crop had generally been stooked for four or five days before the arrival of the threshing outfit. Some farmers had capital invested in a threshing outfit which they used themselves and for threshing the crops of others on a contract basis; so much a bushel or so much an acre or some other measure such as time taken. Some outfits were owned and operated by men who were not farmers. One man I knew who owned a threshing outfit peddled groceries around from farm to farm in the nine months he was not threshing; another ran a livery stable, another was a farm implement dealer.

It was an exciting experience to see the threshing outfit coming. In 1905 the tractors used to supply the energy for threshing were still enormous monsters driven by steam generated by straw burners. A great plume of smoke and steam heralded the coming of the outfit. The great tractor with its enormous broad steel rear driving wheels chugged and clanked over the rough earth roads drawing behind it a train consisting of the separator, a water and fuel cart, a wagon loaded with miscellaneous equipment and sometimes a cook house on wheels.

When the suitable spot for the threshing had been found, usually at a point near the centre of the planted area with some regard to the proximity of the farm buildings and particularly the well, the separator or threshing machine was unhooked, wedges driven under its wheels and the tractor manoeuvred into a position facing its front end. At the other end the giant galvanised sheet iron tube about ten inches across was swung into position sticking up at an angle well above the main body of the machine. From this the straw and chaff were discharged in a tawny yellow deluge. The separator was connected to a driving wheel on the tractor by a large belt about eight inches broad. These were made of horsehide which became a beautiful dark brown in use. Later belts made of canvas and rubber became common, being cheaper, made in lengths requiring only one connecting operation, less liable to breakages and giving better traction.

The tractor and separator constituted the mechanized part of the threshing. The rest was for men and horses and at a greater distance for women who fed and watered the men; a threshing crew numbered from twelve to eighteen men. The tractor required the attention of an engineman and a waterman who supplied straw fuel and water. Both had to keep a sharp look out for fire which was a very real danger on account of the combustible nature of the straw, the frequent need to feed the firebox and the heat generated by the machine as a whole. Then there were two key men; the field pitcher and the spike pitcher. If anyone thought stooking was hard work they only had to become a spike pitcher to know what a man can do in the way of hard work. The field pitcher was the man who followed the wagons carrying sheaves to the separator, and with the assistance of the drivers loaded the wagons. He was armed with a fork with three long steel prongs, which glistened like silver in the sun. The handle was a straight round piece of hard wood about five feet long. With this fork he pitched the sheaves onto the four wheeled wagon drawn by two horses. A bundle wagon had a large open frame approximately eleven feet from top to ground at the back and front and about four feet from the ground in the middle. The field pitcher threw the sheaves onto the wagon and the driver armed with a similar fork arranged them in an orderly pattern to permit quick unloading and to distribute the weight so as to ensure stability of the load.

When the driver reached the separator the spike pitcher climbed on the wagon and began to pitch the sheaves into the feed. This had to be done carefully in order not to foul the knives which cut the binder twine and spread the stalks so that they would pass freely to the header which chopped off the heads so that the main stalk was separated as straw from the ears of grain. These dropped on to a series of tables in rapid motion inside the machine. Fans separated the chaff from the kernels and the final separation took place when the straw and chaff were blown out of the machine and the threshed grain delivered through a moveable metal tube either into jute sacks or into a special wagon called a grain tank, which for some reason was almost always painted green.

Threshing crews were recruited from the farms around and from the itinerant workers like those who travelled the Harvest Specials; miners, people lacking a job "back east", immigrants making a stake on the way to becoming homesteaders or purchasers of land from the C.P.R. or the Hudson's Bay Company, and young men like myself who had "pulled out" of their own

51

community for reasons of pique or restlessness or ambition. Some of the crews from the surrounding farms brought their own horses and wagons, and were accordingly paid more. Labouring men like myself received $1.50 a day plus their board and lodging. This last might mean a camp bed in a barn or in a tent.

A threshing crew expected to be well fed, and they had to be if the men were to work fast enough to harvest the crop before the "freeze up" which could come in Manitoba any time after the first of October and even earlier in Northern Saskatchewan. The first time I went threshing food was provided by the women folk of the farms where we were working and by their friends and relatives. There was a cooperative element about the catering although the farmer himself was expected to provide the bacon, eggs, beef, potatoes, vegetables, fruit, flour, tea, coffee, and sugar which went into the meals. For breakfast to which we sat down about 6.30 a.m. we had porridge with milk and sugar, meat and potatoes, bacon and eggs, bread or sausages and tea or coffee. Dinner came in the middle of the day, and was our principal meal. This was always roast meat, gravy, potatoes, vegetables, pies made of fruit imported from Ontario either fresh or dried, and tea. About four o'clock we had a short break in the fields when lemonade or tea was passed around with a cookie or two. Supper after seven o'clock consisted of cold meat, pickles, fried potatoes and cold pie or bread and jam. Again we had tea.

No alcoholic beverage was ever supplied in my experience, nor were any consumed except perhaps surrepticiously by the man who had to have his "snort". Drinking was done off the job after the harvest was over, and mostly by the itinerant workers when they reached the cities and the bright lights.

Nowadays it has become fashionable to enquire about the sexual activities of almost every conceivable person and community. In the case of threshing crews in 1905, I am obliged to report that there were none. This was something which hap-

52

pened in the cities after the harvest was over. In any event we worked too hard, we ended the day too tired and we got such a real pleasure out of tough, physical activity in the sun and the open air to bother much about sex. A lot of the modern obsession with sex is, in my view, due to the fact that the great majority of men and women are seated all day in offices and at factory assembly lines, and have not the outlets for physical energy and feeling which the great majority of people in the past had when they did hard and often dangerous work together in an atmosphere of freedom and companionship, out of doors, in touch with living things like plants and animals. A spike pitcher had to be a tough, strong and steady man and he had to work ten to fourteen hours a day, and I know from experience that there was real joy in feeling one could do a man's job in the sunshine and the wind in Manitoba in the autumn of 1905. A lot of things seem sick by comparison.

After I had finished stooking with the Beres, I joined the threshing crew run by the Coughlin brothers and their brother-in-law, Ed McKellar. The Coughlins threshed most of the farms in the district, and the crew lived at the farms round about. I stayed the whole time with the McKellar family, and after the threshing was over, I worked for them as a laborer who cut fire wood, harvested the potato crop, and did the general chores, until I had reached that date in November which entitled me to buy a return ticket to Toronto for $5.00. Mrs. McKellar, who was Ed's second wife, was pregnant at the time. Whether this induced a special tenderness in her I do not know, but she was very kind to me. I remember particularly how she looked after me during my first few days with the crew.

My job was to sack oats as they poured out of the spout of the separator. There was nothing much to the job once one learned how to tie a Manitoba knot to close the sack when it was full. But it had one painful drawback. Oats give off a lot of dust in the threshing, and when this mixes with the sweat on one's hands, an abrasive paste is formed which quickly takes off the tender skin between the fingers. After a day or two my hands were raw, but one could not stop or complain. No one ever complained about anything connected with the job of threshing. To do so indicated the character of a sissy or a citified weakling. And so I kept on; sack after sack without cease. Mrs. McKellar saw my hands, and she bathed them and bound them up, and later her husband put me on a different but not softer job. Mrs. McKellar must have felt motherly towards me, for when her baby was born, after I left Manitoba, she named her Ruby Ferns McKellar. Years later I learned that Ruby Ferns McKellar was married to a farmer in south west Manitoba.

4

Early in November, 1905, I returned to London. Within a few days of my arrival home I resumed my apprenticeship as a bricklayer, this time with a building contractor in a modest way of business, Ed Martin. On the 5th of December I had an accident which nearly ended my life. It happened like this.

I was working on a military stores building as an assistant to Fred Northey, Ed Martin's foreman. The building was a plain brick structure three or four storeys in height. The only decorative features of the building were stone lintels over the windows, stone window sills and a belt course of stone which ran around the building at the level of the window heads. At the time of the accident Fred Northey and I were setting the stone course on the second storey. We were, of course, working on a scaffold. Scaffolds are still with us as a necessary part of building operations, and a scaffold in 1905, like a scaffold in 1205, did not differ substantially from the scaffold we see today except that the modern scaffold is made of steel tubes held together by locking devices. Ours were made of poles and planks held together with rope. Then as now the scaffold is given vertical rigidity by fixing a horizontally protruding pole or tube in a gap left in the brick or stone work, which is later filled when the scaffold is removed. The protruding support which fits into this hole was, and perhaps still is, called a putlog. The putlogs are rendered firm in their holes by the weight of bricks, mortar, men and equipment on the scaffold.

In our case the accident happened, as far as I could see, by reducing the weight on the scaffold as Fred Northey and I lifted the stone blocks one by one on to the belt course, resting them on wedges preparatory to trowelling in the mortar necessary to finish off fixing the stone to the bricks beneath. We had lifted the last stone block into place, and were using our strength horizontally to set it square. The weight was off the scaffold and we were pushing horizontally with just enough effort to cause one of the putlogs to come out of its hole. This altered the distribution of weight so that for some reason the scaffold collapsed downwards. Fred Northey and I were pitched straight down 20 feet to the ground. Fred landed on his head, broke his neck and died almost at once. He left a widow and eight children.

I landed on my shoulder and it broke in several places. A number of planks fell on me, and one of the stone blocks, dislodged from the stone course, fell on one of the planks and this shattered my left instep. I was in the hospital for six weeks and I spent another two months of convalescence before returning to my trade.

The aftermath of the accident suggests something of the mean, cheeseparing attitude of big financial enterprises of that time. Ed Martin was, of course, insured against accidents, and under the insurance contracts his workmen were entitled to compensation for injuries. No sooner had I recovered consciousness than my parents and I were being harassed by representatives of the insurance company seeking a settlement on the meanest possible terms. I was too weak to argue, and in any case I was a minor working under indentures. The harassment was then directed exclusively at my parents. My father was too deaf to be affected by the arguments of the insurance man, but my mother, silly woman, capitulated without consulting me and accepted $25.00 as a full settlement.

The settlement offered Fred Northey's widow was so meagre that she took her claim to the courts. Again I was summoned as a witness in a court of the Crown. This time I was more prudent than I had been on my previous appearance on the witness stand. Being an apprentice, new on the job, I claimed that I knew nothing about scaffolds, and whether the one in question was well or ill constructed. Ed Martin had treated me decently and had looked after me in the hospital, and I was determined that he was not going to be blamed by some shyster lawyer employed by a rascally insurance company. In the end, the Court found for Mrs. Northey and awarded her reasonable compensation.

I went back to work on 2nd April, the day of the great fire and earthquake in San Francisco. I served my time with Ed Martin. This lasted until November, 1909. I was paid the standard wages of an apprentice: $1.50 a week during the first year, $3.00 a week during the second; $6.00 a week during the third and $9.00 during the fourth and final year. Thereafter I was a journeyman bricklayer, and a member of the Bricklayers' Union which had its headquarters in Philadelphia in the United States. The rate paid journeymen bricklayers was 70 cents an hour, or $5.60 for an eight hour day. Big money, compared with my father's earnings, but it must be borne in mind that bricklayers did not have steady work, and they were only paid when they were on the job. My father-in-law told me of the time when he was a journeyman in the 1880's. Once he only worked a full 44 hour week on three occasions in a whole year. One of his brothers solved the problem of working as much as he could, by working six or eight months a year in New York and the rest of the year in London, England, where he had his home and where winter work was easier to get on account of the climate. Many bricklayers kept on the move in this way, going wherever it was reported that "things were booming".

After my accident my apprenticeship went smoothly. I learned all aspects of the art of bricklaying, and I could do fancy, fine work like fireplaces. The size of my hands was a handicap. Ideally a bricklayer needs large hands, big, strong wrists and long arms. My father-in-law was so endowed, and he was one of the fastest, neatest men in the business. I remember once my mother-in-law asking him to take the screw top off a jar of preserves, which she could not move. He took the jar in his hands, gave it a twist with such strength that, although the screw top did not budge the glass parted. I did not have this kind of strength, nor a long reach. As a consequence of the size of my hands, I liked cement work better than brickwork, with the result that I never became fast; at least until I was working on my own.

I think my trip to the harvest fields of Manitoba in 1905 had helped me to grow up. That trip was my last rebellion. Thereafter I settled down and began to enjoy life: hard physical work all day; further education; poultry fancying; opera and theatre going; and horse and buggy trips into the country about London.

In order to educate myself I enrolled in the International Correspondence school, the headquarters of which was in Scranton, Pennsylvania. My object was to become an architect. The International Correspondence School was one of the agencies of self help which flourished in North America in the old days. I learned about its existence by reading its advertisements in the *Saturday Evening Post,* a famous magazine published in the United States which contained interesting articles and stories of all kinds, some of them by men whose reputation still stands very high like Joseph Conrad and, in a different way, P. G. Wodehouse. The School was a private enterprise to which one paid fees and from which one received books of instruction and exercises. The exercises were corrected with comments and suggestions. The only entrance requirement was the payment of the fee. The presumption was that no one would pay the fee unless they wanted to learn and could learn. If one was beyond one's depth that was too bad, but no one lost much thereby. I found that mathematics, which I had always hated at school was not beyond me. I actually liked algebra and geometry, particularly geometry. The School paid attention to things like handwriting, and under their direction I began to improve mine. I was not too good at architectural drawing, but I could have mastered this if I had seen the course through. The School gave a diploma, but this meant nothing unless it was backed up by actually being able to do what the diploma suggested one could. Although I never finished the course, or even half of it, I learned a lot from the International Correspondence School. I learned to express myself on paper better than I had ever learned at public school. I learned how to order my thoughts, and how to read something more than a newspaper or a magazine. As far as my own work was concerned I learned how to calculate quantities and to measure things up in a way I never learned as an apprentice bricklayer. Above all I think the course raised my level of aspiration and taught me to see that in order to improve one's lot in life one has to know something in detail and not just to talk about and hope for success or social betterment. When I look back I think I would have done better to stick at my studies than to go for big money quickly, as I did, with all the consequences for me which I shall relate.

To my programme of self education I added poultry fancying. This was a pastime of bricklayers who often had time on their hands on account of bad weather in winter or lack of work. Poultry fancying yielded a few eggs and meat to eat, but in the main fanciers bred "for show". Fancying was for the working man the same kind of thing horse breeding is for the rich. The fancier wanted to show his birds and to win ribbons and medals for breeding males and females with the most perfect plumage and the best appearance of a particular breed.

My fancy was White Orpingtons. I had long read with interest the articles on poultry in the *Farmer's Advocate,* which my father helped to print. I extended my reading to poultry magazines, and I read the advertisements of the great breeders. I bought hatching eggs of which great things were promised, from a man in Illinois who claimed to be one of the top breeders of White Orpingtons.

For me I think poultry fancying was more than something bricklayers did. I had always liked plants, birds and animals and outdoor life. I have always understood animals and birds better than I have understood men and women, and I think I like them better. In my experience people have faculties peculiar to themselves. I have a daughter-in-law, for example, who has the faculty of understanding little children in a most wonderful way. She seems to be able to get into the mind of a small child and think and feel like them so that she understands them. I am like this with animals and birds. It does not mean I am sentimental about them. I have seen born hundreds of thousands of chickens and turkeys, and I have killed probably 20% of this number. If understanding means loving that is how I have been about poultry of all kinds.

Growing up in the early years of this century opened to one a world of entertainment which was almost entirely closed to children. Before the development of the movies, and then radio and television, entertainment derived from watching some sort of spectacle or hearing music; a combination of both was to be found almost exclusively in the theatre, in the opera or the circus. In this matter London was better provided for than most small cities. It is approximately half way between four large cities, Toronto and Montreal to the east and Detroit and Chicago to the west, and on the main railway line between them. In those days theatre and opera companies were obliged to move about the country in search of their audience, and the length of their stopping in any one place depended on the size of the crowds they could attract. London could sustain an opera or theatre company for one or two nights, and so its location between two much larger centres was the principal factor in bringing to the city entertainment of a kind and quality that otherwise it could not have attracted. Londoners were entertained in their own city by Sarah Bernhardt, Ellen Terry, Forbes Robertson and Julia Arthur, performers in their own day of the stature and reputation of Laurence Olivier, Liza Minelli or Peggy Ashcroft today. We saw the famous team of German-American comedians Webber and Fields in the flesh. Every year several of the plays of Shakespeare presented by leading companies were seen in London. Grand operas were performed at least once every season. There was a steady flow

60

of the popular musical comedies: *The Prince of Pilsen, The Quaker Girl, Singalee, The Merry Widow, Chu Chin Chow.* Popular plays like *The Bonny Briar Bush* were presented by travelling stock companies. One of these, The Marks Brothers, made a specialty of socio-political dramas: *Under Two Flags* and *Uncle Tom's Cabin,* which people never seemed to tire of seeing on their annual rounds.

Entertainment of this volume and variety was only possible because London was well provided with two theatres suitably fitted out for the presentation of spectacles like musical comedies and grand opera, and sufficiently large to earn a revenue equal to the cost of "one night stands" by outstanding performers. In the 1890's the only accommodation for opera and theatrical presentations was the auditorium of the Masonic Temple. Just about the turn of the century, however, the Grand Theatre was built on Richmond Street, opposite Saint Paul's Cathedral. This was considered to be one of the best appointed and largest theatres in Canada at the time. It seated some 1,200 people, and it had a large and well equipped stage and lighting system. The audience was divided into three classes, and there were separate entrances for each. I was mainly acquainted with the third class—the gallery gods—to which one ascended by a long, steep, bare stairway, after paying two bits (25 cents) at the entrance..

The second theatre, Bennetts was more modest than the Grand. It was known as the Ten, Twent, Thirt, on account of its admission charges: 10 cents, 20 cents and 30 cents. Bennetts specialized in vaudeville shows, and travelling road companies like The Marks Brothers. Once each week Bennetts held an amateur night, when aspiring actors, jugglers, magicians, singers, comics and acrobats were given an opportunity to show themselves to the public and the talent scouts.

"Going to a show" was a mark of having grown up, of being a man. The height of manhood was achieved when one took a girl to "a show". For the most part, however, young apprentices like myself congregated in the "gods" of the

Grand or in the ten cent seats of Bennetts. Getting a good seat in the Grand was a real struggle. There was no idea of queuing and one used uninhibited physical force to fight one's way up the narrow steep stairs to the gods. When there was a reputedly "good show", one of which news had come via the *Toronto Star* or the *Buffalo Weekly Express,* the struggle for a good seat in the "gods" was like the storming of the Bastille as depicted in *The Illustrated History of the World.*

The voice from the "gods" was a raucous one, and the entertainers, whoever they might be, had to hold the attention of this part of the audience if they were to be heard at all. The character of the shows tended to be determined by the audience. Colour, noise, dramatic entrances, catchy tunes and broad simple jokes were the means of capturing attention and holding it. Audience participation in the amateur nights at Bennets was direct, cruel and effective. If a performer lost the attention of the audience for even a few seconds and boredom seemed about to supervene, a great howl went up, "Get the hook!" Once the volume of howling reached a certain point, the manager in the wings extended a large shepherd's crook and literally hauled the performer off the stage.

It has been said that no one ever lost money underestimating the taste of the people and this was largely so. But we enjoyed ourselves, and it is easy to see why we did so and equally why many intelligent and respectable people took a poor view of the theatre, musical comedies and the like. Not that by modern standards the shows were dirty or morally objectionable. They never sought to justify crime or to glamourize it, nor did they trade in perversion or seek to make natural the unnatural. The shows of those days were designed to work on the imagination by suggestion, and were for this reason more entertaining and exciting than the explicit and boring spectacles which are so often piped into the sitting rooms of the citizen on the T.V. channels. When nothing is left to the imagination, the result is nothing. Fortunately that was not the mode of proceeding of entertainers in the reign of

Edward VII and we used to enjoy ourselves immensely.

Going to the theatre involved some side amusements which I have never heard remarked upon. Many of the occupants of the gods were cigar makers and cigar makers' apprentices. London was then one of the principal centres of the cigar making industry in Canada, a much more important part of the tobacco trade then than now. These workers in the cigar industry used to bring with them to the theatre handfuls of tucks. Tucks were the ends cut off the cigar after the rolling operation was completed. Tucks were consumed either by chewing or by smoking in little clay pipes called daubs. Of course smoking was forbidden in the theatre, and so the tucks were chewed by the young bloods in the gods. Chewing tucks meant the ingestion of strong nicotine, and taken in this way was a considerable intoxicant comparable with pot and some of the drugs we hear so much about today. No one considered chewing tucks was a problem. The practice probably did no real harm very largely because the satisfaction in chewing tucks was more the demonstration of manliness than the pleasure of the activity. Chewing tucks was in fact sickening. Very few young persisted long in the practice. They either graduated to chewing plug tobacco which was much more a ruminant than an intoxicant, or they were put off tobacco altogether. The worst feature of chewing tucks was the continuous and very necessary spitting which was involved. The proprietors of the theatres spread saw dust on the floors to sop up the brown saliva and to facilitate cleaning. Even so the floors became greasy with tobacco juice by the end of an evening. Part of the process of growing up seems to involve a revolt or more often just being revolting, and we teenagers of the 1900's were just as disgusting, I suppose, as similar age groups sixty or seventy years on.

Another aspect of growing up was the experience of getting out of London on one's own, or more often in the company of pals and above all with a girl. There were several ways of getting out of the city. One could go by street car to Springbank Park down the Thames several miles from the centre of the city. Then there was Port Stanley on Lake Erie where there was a beach and where one travelled by the London and Port Stanley Railway, a small electric line which brought to London coal and other heavy materials discharged from lake vessels and provided a popular passenger service for holiday makers. Going to Springbank and Port Stanley was, however, much more a family enterprise than an individual one, and trips out of London to these spots did not compare with the third way of getting out of the city, viz. renting a horse and buggy. This was the man's way.

In every direction from London there were straight dirt roads "along the concessions", i.e. the land given or sold to farmers when this part of Ontario was settled in the late eighteenth and nineteenth centuries. Most farms still possessed a "wood lot" varying in size from a few acres to quite large areas, the "back forty" as they used to say, where the natural forest of Ontario still remained, useful for the shelter of cattle in the summers and a source of fuel, fence railings and even timber. These wood lots often fronted on the roads with the result that one could drive for miles through broken forest along roads lined with maples, oaks, elms, hickory, walnut and birch trees and hazel and chestnut bushes. Bicycling, a pleasure in the city, was not a practical proposition along these roads, which were too dusty and rough for comfort. But in a horse and buggy, what a setting for romance!

The best horse and buggy days were in late September through October. Then the hardwoods were ripe, and the air was filled with fragrance. The leaves of the maples and the birch trees were full of colour. Through most of the morning and the late afternoon a shimmering haze hung over the country. Soft warmth, so different from the fierce heat of the Ontario summer, wrapped you round, and sweet freshness instead of enervating humidity.

In those days there were a number of livery stables in London; in proportion to population probably as many as there are gas stations today. They all rented horses and rigs, and the choice was a wide one. This was a problem, because the horses varied greatly in their characters, dispositions and appearance. One had to know horses or the ostlers who rented them. A skittish or surly horse difficult to manage could spoil an expedition, and failure to drive confidently and masterfully reflected upon one's manhood.

Just as there was a choice of horses, so there was a choice of vehicles. The surrey with a fringe around the top was available, but the preference among the young swains of London was the buggy built for two: a lightly constructed vehicle with a wide, upholstered, well sprung seat, space in the back for a picnic hamper, and a collapsible hood, a protection, when needed, against rain, sun and prying eyes.

An experienced horse understood the purpose of these expeditions into the countryside around London sometimes better, I think, than the human participants. A good horse knew when the mood of the enterprise required a slowing down or a stop. Indeed, I think the horse could create the mood, and all nature worked as one and to advantage.

Of course, horses could work otherwise too. A careless or inexperienced driver, or one to whom a horse might take a dislike, could encounter difficulties and even danger. Let the driver allow the reins to get under a horse's tail, and the discomfited animal might kick in the dashboard. Annoyed or disgruntled with the passengers in the buggy, a horse might get the bit in its teeth and head for home without regard for upsetting the buggy and pitching out the passengers. Fortunately for me I had had a fair amount of experience of horses swamping logs in Algoma and driving Cohoon and Patterson's delivery rig, and so I was able to enjoy the horse and buggy days to the full. But I know it was otherwise with some of my pals who, whatever may have been their way with girls, had no way with horses. In my experience if a horse does not like a man, there is usually a good reason why a woman should not either.

By November, 1909, I had completed my apprenticeship. I

was 21 years old. I had a trade which was worth 70 cents an hour when there was work. I had a bag of bricklayers' tools. I had good health, and a lot of vague ambitions. What would I make of myself? Perhaps I should have thought more about this than I did.

5

In 1909 London was quiet. Life there was smooth and gentle, but it was not exciting. The news from across the Detroit River was that a man named Henry Ford had invented a new kind of automobile which was both cheap and easy to drive. So many people liked his new car and wanted to buy one that he had been obliged to refuse all further orders, until he had built a bigger plant to meet the demand for the new model T. Detroit was the place to find work, and where there is work there is money. This is how I saw the situation in November, 1909.

And so I left London once again; this time forever. Ties of course remained, and as late as 1970 my wife and I had a plot in Woodland Cemetery in London for our final residence. But after November, 1909, I never lived there again. I packed my telescope, strapped up my bag of tools and set out for the place where the action was: Detroit, Michigan, U.S.A.

Two things happened which set me against the United States, and these very soon after leaving Canada; one in fact in crossing the border. Neither had anything to do with economic opportunity, and both revealed to me things about the United States which I could not like.

The first episode concerned my entry into the Republic. In those days there was no particular formality about entering the United States or returning to Canada, but none the less the U.S. Customs and immigration officials watched everyone and picked out the odd one for examination in order to protect the United States from contamination with venereal disease and/or anarchist ideas. I was one picked out for scrutiny. They took me off the train; went through my baggage and tool bag; peered at my private parts and asked some questions about trade unions and politics. I remember once seeing a movie with Paul Newman about a man who was bullied by prison guards. They reminded me of the U.S. officials in Detroit: mean, bullying men who seemed to think that they were somehow doing me a favour by allowing me into their country and that I was coming there to rob them and pollute them. There was nothing in the episode, but it left a nasty taste in my mouth.

The second event which put me off the U.S.A. happened soon after I got a job on the Highland Park plant of Henry Ford. I took a room in a boarding house run by a woman from London, Ontario, Mrs. Clack. She was an Englishwoman who had come to Canada and settled in London before I was born. Her husband had been a drugstore clerk, or, as the English say, a chemist's assistant. He could get no work of the kind which suited him, and in order to keep his wife and four children he took heavy labouring jobs like loading gravel. Being a small, weak man this work killed him. He caught tuberculosis and died. After raising her family Mrs. Clack went to Detroit, rented a large apartment and let rooms and gave meals mostly to English immigrants or to people she knew from London.

One of the Englishmen began to court her only daughter. For some reason he attempted to commit suicide. Today Detroit is the murder capital of the United States, but in those far off days an attempted suicide created a great stir in the newspapers. A day or so after the event I returned to the apartment, rang the bell and was asked by Mrs. Clack over the inter-com to identify myself. I said, "It's Stanley," whereupon several newspaper reporters sprang out of the entrance hallway and began to question me. "Had X attempted suicide because I was trying to get his girl? etc." I told them to go to hell. I did not know X, and did not in fact then know he had attempted suicide. Again there was nothing in the episode but again it left a nasty impression with me of bullying men who seemed willing to do anything and invent anything in order to serve their own purpose. I felt disgusted with the American system.

I worked all winter for Henry Ford in mud and snow at the bottom of a ditch helping to build the brick lining of a great duct for carrying high pressure steam pipes from one part of the Highland Park plant to another. When this job was finished I moved on to Flint, Michigan, where the big Buick plant was being built. I had only been working for a week or so when the foreman beckoned to me. He did not say anything except, "I think you better get what's owing you at the office." I knew the reason. I was not fast enough to suit him.

At that time I was working with a man from London who was much older than I. He proposed that we go to Edmonton, Alberta, where, he had been told, "things were booming", and where there was plenty of work. No sooner said than done, and I was back in Canada, and in the West, where I was to live for the rest of my life.

I arrived in Edmonton shortly before the funeral of Edward VII. I remember this because there was a big funeral parade under the auspices of the Masonic Order with banners and flags edged in black and a band with muffled drums. I went to work on a school. I lasted only a few days. The foreman in Edmonton, like the foreman in Flint, thought I was not fast enough. He fired me. On the 1st of June, 1910, I went to Calgary.

I had heard that a London firm, the McLarey Manufacturing Company was building a warehouse in Calgary, and that the work was being carried out by a London man, George Insell. Insell knew Ed Martin, and in a vague way he knew me. I was a London man, and hence preferable to all others.

Edmonton may have been the capital of the Province of Alberta, then only five years old, but it was a flat boring place compared with Calgary. I have never been able to figure out why Calgary seems to be still, as it was in 1910, the capital of the world as far as I am concerned. God knows I suffered enough heart break in that city, but somehow it is a magic place unlike anywhere else and, for me, totally unforgettable. Probably it was just the fact that I was young and energetic when I first arrived there. Calgary was then a young people's city. You never saw any old people in Calgary. Taking account of the abundance of children and the youth of their parents I would not be surprised to learn from a statistician that the average age of Calgarians in 1910 was about 22 or 23 years. With all this youth, inexperience and energy the atmosphere of optimism was irresistible. Calgary was going to be bigger than Chicago and bigger and better than New York. Comparison with places in Canada was beneath consideration, and in any case there were a lot of Americans in Calgary who would never have made such comparisons.

Of course, nature contributed to this optimism. Far to the west one could see the mighty peaks of the Rockies, and most evenings the vivid sunsets set the blood coursing even after a hard day's work. Alberta was supposed to have everything necessary for success and wealth: coal, gas, oil, minerals, good water, good land, good climate, forests, and the freshest, cleanest air in the world. In the presence of this combination of factors it was easy to forget the fallibility of men and women. We were all young and we were all suckers; some more some less.

When I arrived in Calgary economic development which had begun in a small way after the turn of the century, had become a tremendous and exciting boom. In 1900 there were only 4,000 people in Calgary. By 1910 there were 40,000 and approximately 25,000 of them had arrived since 1905. With an influx of population of these dimensions the building business flourished wonderfully. Tall buildings were sprouting up everywhere in the "down town" area north of the C.P.R. tracks and the station of 9th Avenue. Residential building was speeding ahead creeping up the hills north and south and beyond the

Elbow River. In terms of opportunity Calgary in 1910 was a bricklayer's paradise.

Bricklayers were absolutely indispensable for the construction of large buildings. When the McLarey Warehouse was finished, I worked on the Holy Cross Hospital with Carter Hall Aldinger, one of the biggest firms of engineering contractors west of the Great Lakes. I had not been long in Calgary, however before I discovered the money that could be made by moonlighting. This was the practice of doing additional work on one's own outside the hours prescribed by the Union: in the evenings, Saturday afternoons and even on Sundays. The demand for labour was so great that the men and firms building dwelling houses were prepared to pay individual bricklayers a flat rate of $1.10 a foot, materials found, for the construction of chimneys, and higher rates for fine work on fireplaces. A high proportion of dwelling houses in Calgary were built at that time of the cheapest building material available, lumber, and various saw mill products like shingles. But all required chimneys, and this involved about 35 feet of brickwork from the floor of the basement to a point beyond the ridge of the roof of a two storey dwelling house. The pay for building a chimney was, thus, approximately $35.00, and the work could be done in eight to ten hours. Working for myself I could make as much on a weekend as I made in a week working for a big building contractor.

This got me into trouble with the Union. I was called before an official and, after hearing him out I gave him my union card and told him to do with it what is indicated by a reverse V-sign. While a union may do some workers in big industries some good at some time I believed then, and I still believe, that unions are the means through their agreements with employers of keeping the wage worker in his place, i.e. keeping him always a wage worker with no hope of ever doing better than the union allows him to do and the bosses want him to. The main effect of union activities is to preserve a substantial body of men and women who have neither the inclina-

71

tion nor the ability to be anything but slaves; not slaves whom their masters buy and sell and flog and flay, but people who are obliged to sell themselves. Unions are big organizations. The Bricklayers' Union was, and maybe still is, something with headquarters in Philadelphia, which could oblige one to go out on strike in Calgary, Alberta, about something I had never heard of and could not care less about. As a big organization the Union supported other big organizations which were interested in what they called the supply of labour. The possibility of a man being his own master was and is thus diminished. One of my sons has travelled a lot in South America and he tells me that in Buenos Aires the men who drive buses run their own bus lines, make a good living and are free and self-sufficient people. That illustrates what I mean. Workers can be free and independent if they emancipate themselves from big organizations and big government. That was how I felt then when the Union tried to stop me working for myself and that is how I still feel, and I say this in the full knowledge that by trying to be a free, independent bricklaying contractor I fell flat on my face; this story will show how.

When I quit the Union late in 1910, I joined forces with a man from Fergus, Ontario, named Ed Humphries. He was about fifteen years older than I, and an extremely hard worker. He was a married man with three children, two of whom were crippled by polio. We formed a kind of partnership. I say kind of partnership, because, although we were partners and friends, we were both innocent of business experience and we had no formal agreements about anything. An example of our arrangements is provided by our method of paying ourselves. We had a joint account in the Standard Bank, and each of us took what he needed without any agreement about who got what and when. Our only business principle was to pay promptly our bills for supplies—bricks, sand, lime, fodder for our horse etc. I kept such accounts as we had, and Ed Humphries borrowed some of my books from the International Correspondence School, in order to learn something about estimating quantities of materials required for buildings.

For a time after my arrival in Calgary, I kept up with my work for the International Correspondence School, but soon money became more attractive than study. Short term gains prevailed over long term prospects. If my energies had been devoted entirely to the affairs of Humphries and Ferns, brick-laying contractors, this would not have been so bad. As things developed, however, I abandoned study for land speculation.

Not long after I established myself in Calgary I ran into a young man of about my own age from London: Alger Hart. He was the son of an ex-British soldier who had settled in London. For some reason or other the Harts were regarded as a "rough" family, and, although I knew Alger Hart as a boy, the youngsters on William Street had but little to do with the Harts or the boys they associated with. Alger's mother was a Christian Scientist, which in the 1890's was regarded as an eccentric and strange religious enthusiasm. Alger himself was a handsome, virile young man who was a clerk in a dry goods store. He had charming manners and an easy, attractive way with women which not infrequently ended up in extra-mural adventures in the secluded corners of the park on Prince's Island in the Bow River. But mainly he was interested in land speculation.

He and I shared a room in Mrs. Twombley's boarding house. In the evenings we used to stroll along Eighth Avenue from Second Street East westwards. Every second building seemed to house a real estate office offering land for sale in and around Calgary. The men who had bought up blocks of land had sub-divided them into city lots intended for building pur-poses. Already land values in the centre of the town had risen to great heights, and tales were told of the vast profits which had come to the lucky people who had owned land where Eighth Avenue now ran, and of those who had even made a killing on land along Twentieth Avenue West and in Mount Royal, where the grand homes of the new rich were being built. The real estate business was very democratically organ-

73

ised. A man could buy a pair of city lots for $250. One did not have to pay cash: only $40 down and the rest in instalments due in three months, six months, and nine months. The demand for lots was fueled by the exuberant optimism which seemed well founded upon the evidence of the eye: all those buildings, some of them skyscrapers of ten or fifteen storeys, and houses which were sprouting up everywhere. Ed Humphries and I were building some of the chimneys and fireplaces; we were being paid $135 to $150 for each job. This was real; our work was real.

As the demand for lots increased so the price of them rose. Alger Hart and I were picking up $100, $200, $300 on lots we never really owned outright. We sold lots long before we had paid for them, and pocketed our profits. It would have been all right if we had actually pocketed our profits. But we did not. Profits went into more down payments. We had lots, unpaid for, in Glengarry, South Calgary, Balmoral, Regal Terrace, Sunnyside, Westmount and on the Walker Estate. We did business with Colgrove Brothers, for whom we built chimneys and fireplaces. The senior Colgrove already had a mansion in Mount Royal with a ballroom decorated with gold leaf. When the crash came the Colgroves offered to pay for some of their chimneys with land.

This was the state of the play during 1911 and 1912. Humphries and Ferns were working all hours killing themselves building chimneys and fireplaces in Calgary. On occasions they ventured outside Calgary on big jobs. For example they once did the brickwork on an elaborate ranch house near Bassano, Alberta. During that job the huge thigh bone of a dinosaur was uncovered while digging the well for the ranch. But mainly Humphries and Ferns were helping to build the houses springing up like weeds on the bald headed prairie and hills of Calgary. If the foreman on the Buick plant in Flint, Michigan, had thought young Ferns slow, Bill Leighton who carried the hod for him in Calgary did not. He complained that the pace was too fast; so fast that he quit and took a job as a milkman.

After the crash Bill Leighton offered to get me a job as a milkman.

In 1910 in Calgary it was still feasible to feel the wilderness in the way one feels it in the books of James Fennimore Cooper or in the work of Francis Parkman. There were many Indians about. The edge of the Sarcee Reserve was but a few miles from the Calgary city boundary. Not only this, but some people still ate wild game as part of their diet. When I first arrived in Calgary I shared a room in Mrs. Twombley's boarding house. The Twombleys were an American family originally from New England. Twombley and his son ran a shooting gallery in down town Calgary, and Mrs. Twombley took in boarders. Mr. Twombley and his son were great hunters, and we were served for dinner at one time or another the roast, fried or grilled flesh of most every species of animal at large in the foot hills of the Rocky Mountains. On one occasion the Twombley's boy returned with a wagon load of wild geese all shot on the edge of a slough south of Calgary. They sold them in their shooting gallery for 25 or 30 cents a piece.

Not only was Calgary an exciting place on account of rapid development, the speculative boom, the splendours of nature and the smell of the wilderness, but because the people were proud of themselves and manifested this pride in a great spectacle, The Calgary Stampede. Most Canadian cities had an annual festival of work and production, in the form of a Fair, at which people enjoyed themselves congregating together to eat, drink, gamble, ride on ferris wheels and merry-go-rounds and to examine the results of the work of the community and to discover who made the best butter, raised the best wheat, bred the best cattle or built the best tractor. The Western Fair in London was always a big event in the London year. Calgary, too, had a fair of a kind, but then in 1911 it was proposed that in 1912 Calgary hold in addition to the traditional fair, a great exhibition of the skills and games and way of life of the ranching frontier, the Calgary Stampede.

The Calgary Stampede is still a great spectacle but none of the annual shows have equalled the Stampede of 1912 as an uninhibited, exciting and total exhibition of ranching and frontier life. The men who conceived of the first Stampede planned no ordinary rodeo bringing together a few Alberta cowboys to see who could ride an unbroken horse the longest. The organizers of the first Stampede brought together every element in the life of the range from Mexico to the North West Territories. Indians, half breeds and the whites were brought together each with their own opportunity to display their skills and show off their way of life. Nobody came to the Stampede as a participant with cap in hand. All came on their horses and took over the town.

For the Indians the Stampede was an opportunity to resume briefly the nomadic life of their ancestors, for they left their reservations en masse as tribes, and moved along the trails to Calgary, where they encamped about the city. There were four great tribes in southern Alberta: the Sarcees, the Blackfeet, the Bloods and the Stoneys, and they all moved on Calgary with their squaws and their children and their horses and their cattle. They all dressed up in their very best, and the Indian's very best was splendid. Ordinarily nobody envied the Indians, and most of them looked lonely and depressed, but dressed up for the Stampede moving together as a society they were an impressive sight and their teepees and camp fires a source of unsettling wonder.

Another feature of the total spectacle was the great company of Mexican *vaqueros* who came from the great ranching states of Sonora, Chihauhua and Durango. In some ways they were more dramatically impressive than the Indians, both on account of their costumes and their elegant horsemanship. Each *vaquero* wore an enormous sombrero with tiny red pom poms hanging from the rim. The harness of their horses was ornamented with brightly burnished, solid silver, and their velvet jackets and leather chaps likewise. Their great spurs were of silver and so were the ornaments on their boots. There was no *vaquero* who did not ride a beautiful and spirited horse. I can still see as a vivid memory the leading *vaquero* riding at the head of the procession before the officials of the Stampede and the great crowd in the stands. As he sat easily on his high stepping and restive horse he disdainfully rolled a cigarette in one hand, put it in his mouth and lit it all in one elegant, flourishing motion without in any way relaxing his hold over the reins in his other hand with which he controlled his taut and spirited horse.

The Stampede was a spectacle, but it was also an exhibition of the skills of cowboys organized as competitive sport. The chuck wagon race is a good example of this. Loading up the cooking equipment wagon of working cowboys engaged in branding, driving or disinfecting cattle is a job involving some skill, and so is driving the chuck wagon. The idea of seeing who could load a chuck wagon, stow the gear snugly enough to stand a rough, fast drive, and then drive the chuck wagon over a measured course in the least time converts a working skill into a means of sport and entertainment. That is just what a chuck wagon race is with plenty of comic possibilities as well as dangers.

Similarly other skills of cowboys in breaking horses, roping steers and calves, branding cattle and driving them were converted into sports. The ranches around Calgary provided a good supply of unbroken horses, bucking broncos, and the cowboys were expected to demonstrate how long they could stay on one of these critters and whether they could master one in a given time. Riding broncos was often a contest not just among cowboys, but between cowboys and horses. There were some horses which could not or would not be broken to riding, and these were the real test of a cowboy's skill as a rider. There was one celebrated horse named Midnight, which was the final challenge for cowboys, and the announcement that so and so was going to ride Midnight was a guarantee of a real display like Ali vs Frazier.

The steers and calves of the Alberta ranches differed in no

way from steers and calves elsewhere. In order to ensure drama and danger the organizers of the Stampede in 1912 imported a supply of Texas longhorns. These never seemed to me practical commercial animals, but for the purpose of testing the courage and skill of the *vaqueros* and cowboys they were ideal. They had huge long horns sharp as needles, and lean muscular bodies which enabled them to run like greyhounds. Roping and tying them was a difficult and dangerous business both for the cowboy and his horse. Bull dogging, the art of grappling with the steer and throwing him down as might be the case in branding was even more difficult and dangerous. Bull dogging involved great strength, skill in using one's weight against the superior strength and weight of the animal and tremendous courage and will power. Some of the *vaqueros* and cowboys, locked in combat with a steer, would inflict enough pain on the creature to break its will to resist by sinking their teeth into the steer's nose. This was real savagery which makes us one with the animals, and there was nothing synthetic or contrived about it as it was displayed in the Calgary Stampede in 1912. Nowadays, of course, the cowboy is obliged to display the skill necessary to place a ribbon over the steer's horns, but he is not challenged in life and will as the *vaqueros* and cowboys were in the first Calgary Stampede.

Rough sport of this kind was hard on the participants, both men and animals. Bones were broken and blood shed on both sides. I do not know whether any men were killed in 1912, but a few were seriously injured. As for the animals, they were dragged off and slaughtered when their bones were broken, and their carcasses were taken by the Indians to provide the means of their feasting.

To me the Calgary Stampede of 1912 was a marvellous event. It was colourful, dramatic and thrilling, and all this was rooted in the real life of work and reliance upon human qualities like courage and skill. And it was a display open to everyone: Indians, Mexicans, Americans and Canadians. It brought the life of nature into the city in a much more real way than one can by building a zoo or showing motion pictures or engaging in play acting. Some people may say the Calgary Stampede was savage and cruel. I do not think so. To me it was a splendid event, which, after all is said about the excitement and drama, left one with a knowledge of what it is to be a human being.

At the time I needed this knowledge more than I could ever suspect was possible. I was caught up in the excitement of Calgary and flowing with optimism. When I was not slugging it out with bricks and mortar, I was making a fortune out of land speculation. By the autumn of 1912 I figured I was worth at least $10,000. I was a partner in a thriving business. I was on the way up in the best town in the world. Look at those mountains! Breathe that fresh air! Feel those warm Chinooks blowing through the passes from the Pacific! Boy, oh, boy! I had the world by the tail. Twenty-five years old, and on our way! Up! It was then that I decided to marry.

6

Just before Christmas, 1912, I returned to London, Ontario. On the 4th of March, 1913, Janie Sing and I were married in the Cronyn Memorial Church where we both had been baptized, had gone to Sunday School, had been confirmed and and had worshipped. For our honeymoon we travelled through the United States by way of Chicago and Minneapolis to Winnipeg, and from there by the Grand Trunk to Edmonton and finally by the C.P.R. to Calgary. We brought with us furniture for our home: carpets from Kidderminster, china from Limoges, chairs upholstered in leather from Spain, silver, bedroom furniture of gum wood from Central America, and pots and pans manufactured close to home in London, Ontario. We moved into the house which Alger Hart and I had bought and mortgaged on 20th Avenue West, to which the citizens had attempted to give the name of Royal Avenue.

20th Avenue may have led to Mount Royal and the blessed abodes of the new rich. For me it led nowhere. Between my departure for London, Ontario, in December, 1912, and my return to Calgary late in March, 1913, the bottom had dropped out of everything in Calgary. The Mackie Building, an intended sky scraper, was a great framework of steel on which no one worked, and on which no one ever again worked until it was torn down for scrap. My fortune in land worth an estimated $10,000 was not worth 10,000 cents. Far from it. My holdings had a negative value inasmuch as I owed money on uncompleted contracts to purchase.

Our contracting business was contracting in the real sense of that word. We had begun to owe money for labour and materials, and people owed us money for work done. Before I returned to London, Ontario, I had transferred the books of Humphries and Ferns to Ed Humphries. I never saw them again. Ed and his wife were friendly and kind to me and my wife, but things had changed, and the undefined nature of our partnership became more undefined. We did not even know how to go bankrupt.

If I knew then what I know now, I should have pulled up stakes, and gone elsewhere—perhaps back to London, Ontario; at least to some place where things were better than in Calgary. I should have just left like hundreds and thousands of others; left everything. But I stayed. I still believed in Calgary. I still believed in myself. I still believed in the West. In fact I could not believe I was beaten, and I did not want to face failure, for in those days no one believed that a society could fail. Only individuals failed. I had not been smart enough. And that I could not face. Furthermore I believed that a man should pay his debts. I humiliated myself by borrowing $300 from my parents and $600 from my wife's parents in order to pay final instalments on lots which remained open prairie for forty years, and which were subsequently seized for unpaid taxes.

Through 1913 and 1914 until the spring of 1915 Ed Humphries and I continued to do some work. House building had stopped in Calgary, but there were a few jobs to be found outside the city. The coming of war brought a feeble revival of industrial and commercial building, but nothing sufficient to save us, and in any case we did not have the capital to undertake big jobs when there were any. People owed us money and we owed everyone. We fell further and further behind. Ed Humphries abandoned the enterprise. I never discovered how he did it, but he managed to get a bonding company to bond him in order that he could take a job with an oil company.

Meanwhile my responsibilities had not lessened. In December, 1913, our first son was born in our house on 20th Avenue, West: a bloody business superintended by an incompetent butcher who was late for his game of bridge. I am sure my Granny Dickens would have done better and behaved better.

Sometimes I think I was a soft mug. I was paying Alger Hart rent for the house in which I lived because he was a part owner. I was also paying off my share of the mortgage. There was, however, a saving element in this because the man looking after the mortgage on behalf of a relative eventually used his influence to get me a job which would enable me to keep up the mortgage payments.

In the spring of 1915 the end came as far as contract brick-laying was concerned. By August I was so broke, I was obliged to store our household belongings and send my wife and son back to her parents until I got back on my feet. When I put my wife and son on the train going east I gave the sleeping car porter a dollar with the injunction that he look after them well. It was the last dollar I had.

When I look back on my experience I can see now that Calgary was dead, and remained so for nearly forty years. Twenty percent of the houses were empty. Stores were boarded up. The life of the place depended on the activity of the railroads and the packing houses and the warehouses handling supplies for ranchers and farmers. The town was overbuilt for the level of real productive enterprise in that part of the province, and this condition continued for many years. There was a revival of hope based on the discovery of oil in Turner Valley, but this never measured up to expectation. And yet faith in Calgary and Alberta was justified forty years on, and today, Calgary is the city of the dreams of the suckers of 1905–1913. Where I failed my second son succeeded in the 1950's and 1960's so well that he has been able to drop out in his early 50's to build the kind of life out of doors which was always my best aspiration.

As soon as my wife and son were on the train towards the safe security of London, Ontario, I headed for the harvest fields. My first job was stooking for the Honan brothers who had a big spread near Alderside, Alberta. From there I joined the threshing crew of an outfit run by two American brothers. For their foreman they employed another American from Indiana named Fuss, who worked for the rest of the year for the Honans. Fuss was a skilful, hard working man, but he conformed to my idea of an American in authority. He was a bully and a brute. He sneered at me when he discovered I did not know how to hitch a four horse team. I had to bite my tongue and clench my fists in order not to give him as good as he gave, and he never succeeded in provoking me to fight him. This represented no triumph of self control on my part. I needed a job and I needed money, and so I shut up. Not so others, and Fuss succeeded in fighting and firing more than one man in the crew.

It was ten years since I had first gone harvesting. In that time there had been technical progress and human retrogression. The tractors were now powered with gas engines, but they were still giants in size. This outfit had an "Oil Pull", a famous name among tractors in 1915. The separators were now larger, and the spike pitchers had to work even harder than in 1905. Pay was up. We got $2.00 a day. But the friendly family atmosphere which I had known in 1905 was gone. We lived in a tent. The meals were prepared by a hired cook. They were as abundant as ever, but they were badly prepared. In the grub tent there were tables with which Charlie Chaplin could have done wonders. They were circular, and in the middle there was a revolving platform bearing the food for the crew. One grabbed what one wanted or what one could get as the platform was pushed around by the diners.

Breakfast was such a greasy mess that it turned my stomach. All I could take was some of the ill cooked porridge, a few hunks of bread and the coffee which was little better than swill. As a result I was ravenously hungry by noon. I used to work around so that when the dinner gong sounded, I was the first into the grub tent. Fuss used to ride me about this, but I got a good helping of meat and potatoes.

In spite of the general atmosphere of slavery which the American owners and their foreman contrived to create, the men were cheerful enough when they were together at meals or resting after dusk before hitting the hay. Because of the supposed constipating properties of cheese it was commonly called binder. But Massey Harris made the binders used in cutting the crops, and so cheese which the wits had called binder became Massey Harris. "Spin us some Massey Harris," a man would say in order to get the revolving platform moved in his direction. There was a German speaking Swiss in the crew who was hired with his team of horses. His English was very limited, and he came to believe that the English for cheese was Massey Harris. Some years later when I was in the Alderside district I heard the story of how a crazy Swiss had once asked in a grocery store for some Massey Harris, and had been sent to the farm implement dealer.

With wit like this livening up our intercourse we never lacked for amusement. There was a Welshman in the crew named A. G. Evans. The initials on his suitcase were A.G.E. He was therefore called "Century", and the men used to ask him what it was like a hundred years ago or why he did not cut his white beard. Unfortunately Evans was infested with lice, and when he shared a tent with me I became infested, too. When I returned to Calgary in late October after the harvest I was as lousy as a pet coon. The first thing I did was to go to the hotel, rent a room, take a long, hot bath and throw my underwear and socks out of the hotel window on to the roof of an adjoining building. I dug out some pyjamas which had never been unpacked on the harvest, put them on under my suit, and went out to re-equip myself with clean underclothing.

During the last ten years or so I have been asked several times about the existence of homosexuality among men in threshing gangs, logging camps and such like. For most of my life I had never heard of the word, and I had an almost equal ignorance of the activity which the word denotes. This threshing crew provided an instance of something which at the time I did not quite understand. There were two brothers in the crew —green Englishmen from Walthamstow, a part of London, England, and it was whispered and hinted that one ought to steer clear of them or one might get one's sleep disturbed. I, personally, never saw or experienced anything to suggest that they were any different from the other fellows, but there was a very distinct and hostile feeling about them among the threshing gang as a whole. If there was homosexuality among gangs of workers on the farms, in the mines and in the lumber camps of Canada I never saw any evidence of it during my time. But I suppose homosexuality is like much else; it is a case of seek and ye shall find. I never did.

When I was finally paid off I had nearly $200.00 Just after pocketing it I encountered the foreman, Fuss, with some other men. He made a last, nasty remark to me and I turned to him and said: "Goodbye, you stupid, hillbilly son of a bitch." He made a move to tackle me, but the other men said things like "That goes for me, too," and "Hear, hear," whereupon Fuss turned away cursing in a kind of high whine. This can be said for Americans, like Fuss; they do pay attention to public opinion once they have not got the upper hand.

When I arrived back in Calgary, I had to find a job. This was one of those occasions when I prayed for a break. I was determined that I would never beg for money or borrow outside the circle of my family. Rather than do that I would join the army. This was the way out which many men in my circumstances were taking at this time. I did not want to join the army for a number of reasons. The idea that somehow the Germans threatened Canada and threatened me did not make any sense. I felt no impulse to seek adventure. I had a wife and child to look after, and I wanted to re-establish a home. Furthermore I had promised my wife that I would never join up. I did not like the idea of being ordered about by people who were probably like Fuss. I might, too, have been rejected on

85

account of having broken my instep. In spite of all this, I decided, however, that if I did not get a break I would try to enlist in the 85th, which was the regiment being recruited in Calgary at that time. But my prayer was answered. I got a job on the Hump, i.e. the yards of the C.P.R. where freight trains were made up for their several destinations. This was a real answer to prayer and the gift of salvation because the men of the 85th were nearly all massacred in the battle of the Somme.

I found that working on the Hump, if not as likely to end my life as soldiering on the Somme, was dangerous enough. In the first place the work of making up freight trains was done at night. During the winter of 1915–16 there was some very severe weather in Calgary; temperatures as low as -30 F, with the consequence that there was always snow and ice underfoot. In slippery conditions in the dark my job was to throw a switch so that a rolling freight car would coast down a short incline to join with other freight cars to make a train destined to Vancouver or Edmonton or Lethbridge, or eastward towards Regina, Winnipeg, North Bay, Toronto or Montreal. The cars were shunted by a yard engine from their various points of loading or arrival to the Hump, so that gravity would carry them to their destination on, for example, the Seaboard track where the freights for Vancouver were coupled together and sent on their way, or other tracks to Edmonton etc. The first sorting was made at the bull switch which directed the rolling cars to a preliminary classification of tracks and the next switch, according as it was thrown, would make the final sorting. Each freight car was ridden by a brakeman, who swung on to the car at the bull switch or earlier, mounted a ladder to a platform in front of the wheel with which the brakes were applied manually. He was armed with a heavy wooden stick like a baseball bat which he thrust into the spokes of the brake wheel to give him great leverage as he applied the brakes. This he had to do in order to arrest the forward motion of the heavy cars, having a laden weight of as much as 60–70 tons.

Braking like this in the dark was a matter of skill, physical strength, judgment and agility. Too sharp a collision could cause damage and throw the brakeman from his perch 20 feet or so above the ground. Too quick an arrest of the car prevented the automatic couplings from working, and a gap would be left in the train which would otherwise have to be closed by using a locomotive. There was always some sort of a jarring bang when the cars met and their couplings closed together, but the brakeman's object was to reduce this to a satisfying click which spoke of an exact and sufficient application of the brakes. In order not to be thrown off or bruised by the jarring collision of the cars which up to a point was almost inevitable, the brakemen developed the knack of jumping at the exact moment of impact so that they were momentarily in the air when the rolling car came into contact with the stationary one in front of it. I admired tremendously the skill and daring of the brakemen, and I hoped for an opportunity to try my hand at this job.

We worked in perishing cold and under conditions which required a high degree of concentration. To throw the switch incorrectly and hook up a car for Edmonton to a train for Vancouver meant an elaborate time wasting journey for the Yard master. Too many mistakes and you were fired. The signals were made by lantern, and one simply had to understand their exact meaning. When there was a break in the work, the switch men and brakemen crowded into a tiny shack, not much bigger than a privy, where a great coal fire soon produced a sweat on a man. Sweating, but grateful for warmth, we then had to face the wind and frost outside. Why we did not all die of pneumonia, I shall never know.

I can understand the feeling many people have about railways. The giant power of the locomotive, the size of the cars, the far places to which they go, the idea of a lonely ride night and day across the vast wilderness of Canada, all these make for fascination. I should have half liked to become a "railroader". I applied to take the tests for a trainman in the hope that some day I might work up to the prestigious and well paid post of conductor, than whom there was no more important man on the railway except the locomotive engineers and the head office executives.

But I failed the colour tests. I could distinguish the primary colours accurately and easily enough, but when confronted with a table covered with wisps of wool of a hundred different shades I was not quick enough in distinguishing colours like mauve from a shade of pink or very pale green from very pale yellow. The railways demanded super-perfection in the running trades, and I think they were absolutely justified in this. Railway men were paid not just for effort, but for being right as often as was humanly possible.

At this time I was living a life of extraordinary simplicity and economy. In my room I had a small kerosene stove. On this I prepared a pot of thick porridge. I ate some of this with milk and sugar for breakfast. The rest I dumped into a bowl and let it set firm. For my other meals I sliced the solid cold porridge and fried it. To this I added a small flat tin of Clark's pork and beans which could then be bought for five cents. In this way I nourished myself and saved money.

When I failed to secure a permanent job on the railway, I went to see a man named Dolan. He was the principal of the high school in Calgary, the Central Collegiate Institute. Dolan looked after the mortgage on the house on 20th Avenue West, which was "owned" jointly by Alger Hart and myself. He had the same interest I had in my having a job and an income. He used his influence to have me taken on as an assistant janitor of the Collegiate at $50.00 a month. On the strength of this I rented a house on 11th Avenue N.E. on the North Hill and sent for my wife and son. I managed to earn extra money doing carpentry work on the weekends and in the evenings helping to erect stands for the Calgary Fair and Stampede, and I did a few bricklaying jobs ouside Calgary building foundations for barns.

No sooner had I a job than creditors began to gather like

vultures to see what pickings there were. To most I could only suggest that if they could collect money owing to me they could have it to satisfy my debts. This argument was accepted, but not in the case of two men whom I only knew as Charlie and George. They were Cockney immigrants who had worked for me as labourers. I owed them fifty or sixty dollars in unpaid wages. A lawyer who specialized in such matters got for them an order to garnishee my wages. Thus, I was supporting my family and paying two other men. Charlie and George were the type of English who regard an employer as a natural enemy, and in dealing with him they ought to work as little as possible and get from him as much as possible on the theory that anyone who accepts any kind of responsibility and gives any kind of an order is a man of property and therefore a fair target in class warfare. Long after I had paid them off Charlie appeared one day at my home, and claimed I still owed him $25.00. He seemed to think that anyone living in more than one room somehow ought to share his property with him. I told him to go to hell, and warned him that if he ever showed his face around my place again I would give him a thrashing. He was the sort of man who caused Canadian employers to put up the signs one used to see before World War I "No Englishmen need apply".

The head janitor of the Collegiate Institute was a man who appeared to have learned from the school teachers the proposition: the devil finds work for idle hands to do. In order to protect me from the vice of idleness he ordered me, for example, not only to shovel all the snow off the school walks, but to shovel the snow off all the sidewalks around the perimeter of the school grounds. He demanded that I do this even when a Chinook wind was melting the snow as fast as I could shovel it. He was not, however, all seeing, and on one occasion while working in the loft under the roof of the school I discovered an effort made, probably by some disgruntled student, to burn down the school. A garland of matches was tied around a steam pipe of the heating system and under the garland was a mixture of sawdust and matches. I reported this directly to the Principal.

Shortly after this Mr. Dolan arranged for me to become the head janitor of Riverside School, one of the older schools of Calgary. This was possible because in 1916 the School Board decided to open one of the great and elegant schools built on the North Hill during the epoch of optimism which ended in 1913. The head janitor of Riverside School was transferred to Stanley Jones School, named after one of Calgary's war heroes.

Stanley Jones School serves to illustrate the ideas of public magnificence which were entertained by Calgarians. The school stood on the brow of the North Hill looking across a partially developed subdivision of Riverside in the valley of the Bow River. It was constructed of beautiful sand stone cut and built by the finest craftsmen. The classrooms had twenty foot ceilings and the floors were of the finest polished hardwood. The roof was made of slate imported from Wales. The foundations were of high quality granite. A portrait in oils of Captain Stanley Jones hung in the entrance hall. Sandy Bruce, the janitor, guarded this palace with the greatest of care, polished it till it shone, and saw that no child ever stepped out of line above the level of the basement or ever defaced or damaged any scrap of its surface.

My own school was a more modest establishment. My job was to keep it clean and warm. I was obliged to arrive early in order to bring the temperature of the gas fired heating system up to an acceptable level by 8:30 a.m. Cleaning was carried out after the close of school at 4:00 p.m. There were a number of jobs of routine maintenance and repair. On the whole the life of a janitor was not arduous, although the hours were long and I had much time on my hands. And so I went back to school. In the early morning I used to practise handwriting on one of the blackboards, executing the exercises prescribed in the handwriting manuals which in those days were part of pupils' equipment. I learned a perfect free hand, and my Italian long hand was, by the time I ended this phase of schooling, pretty fair. Handwriting was an art before World War I which students were expected to master and most did. Legible handwriting was only then ceasing to be a required skill of anyone seeking office work. The notion that good handwriting was a mark of education lingered on, so that I thought of it as an accomplishment. Both my wife and I at the age of eighty-five write a much better hand—more legible, more regular and more beautiful to look at than some of our university educated children.

In the hours when school was in session I began to read books from the school library. This was the first time I had ever read anything except the *Saturday Evening Post,* the *Farmer's Advocate,* the *Christian Herald*, boys books by Henty, and the instructional volumes of the *International Correspondence School.* In the furnace room of Riverside School in Calgary I read a good part of Dickens, Victor Hugo's *Les Miserables,* the journals of Lewis and Clark's expedition to the Oregon country, the lives of several British statesmen and the life of Abraham Lincoln. What surprised me was that I liked to read something besides newspapers and magazines, but I am afraid I never followed up this interest systematically. I was always too busy making a living until I was past seventy. Perhaps I should have remained a janitor to become learned, but I did not.

Our next door neighbour on 11th Avenue North East was Warren Hastings. This was a name I remembered my grandfather Ferns talking about, and I looked up some facts about the man who had made the name famous in India and in England. My neighbour Warren Hastings was also a young Englishman who was overseas, but he was managing the Fry's Cocoa Company's sales office in Calgary. He was a large, energetic man who drank a great deal. I remember the way he went about gardening. He dug up the remains of the prairie in his back yard. He raked it energetically, and planted a great variety of seeds. The seeds did not germinate fast enough for his liking. He strode home with a watering can. After using it for half an hour, he set off downtown again and returned with 100 feet of garden hose. He drenched the garden for a few nights, and then he lost interest in his dilatory vegetables, and turned once more to the bottle.

His wife was a pretty young woman named Phyllis who had once been a music hall artist in England with Fred Karno's circus. She used to tell us about Charlie Chaplin, who was by 1916 well known as a movie star. She had not known Chaplin, but she had seen him perform when he was still a child. She said he had a wonderful power to interest and amuse an audience even when very young. Phyllis Hastings was a somewhat indifferent housekeeper, but she was a lively woman. My eldest son tells me that the earliest memory he has is one of sitting with his mother in front of a log fire listening to Phyllis Hastings singing a sad song. Her life was a sad one, too. Eventually she separated from her husband, taking with her her only daughter. She worked in Winnipeg for some years as a clerk in the Hudson Bay Company's department store. She had many illnesses and died in Winnipeg nearly forty years ago. Warren Hastings turned up at her funeral still as large as life and twice as natural.

While we were neighbours of the Hastings we were paying $15.00 a month rent. I heard of an even cheaper house closer to my work. It was, like many houses in Calgary, empty, and I had a difficult time finding someone from whom I could rent it. When I did I ran into another difficulty. I had to pay my present landlord rent before moving out, and my new landlord the rent of the cheaper house before I moved in. I had no money in the bank, and my pay cheque came on the moving day after the banks were closed. I tried to get my old landlord to give me one day's grace. But no. He threatened me with the bailiffs, and I began to understand Dickens better than ever. Somehow I untangled this one and we moved. And just as well I had less rent to pay, because my wife had to go into the hospital where one had also to pay cash.

One day in the summer of 1917 I read an advertisement in the *Calgary Herald* in which it was stated that the Immigration Department of the Canadian Pacific Railway required a manager for the poultry department of their Demonstration Farm at Strathmore, Alberta. Somehow bricklaying and building had ceased to seem a way of life for me. In wartime in other parts of Canada there was plenty of work of this kind to do, but for some reason I never contemplated moving away from Alberta in search of new opportunities in my trade. I never regarded being a school janitor as anything but a temporary way of making ends meet. What was it that prompted me to read that advertisement and take it seriously? I was no more qualified to manage a poultry farm than I was to manage a bank, and yet I thought that this was something I wanted to do. I applied for the job.

Perhaps it was my improved handwriting which prompted the head of the Immigration Department, J. G. Rutherford, to call me for an interview. He himself wrote a beautiful hand, and his signature was a work of art in itself, clear, bold and finely formed. He asked me how long I had been interested in poultry. I replied, "All my life."

"Well," said Mr. Rutherford, "that can't have been long."

What it was which induced J. G. Rutherford to employ me I do not know. Perhaps it was because I could tell one breed from another. Perhaps it was because I knew what poultry ate. Perhaps it was because I knew how they were bred. Perhaps it was because I talked the jargon of a poultry farmer. I soon found, however, that I knew absolutely nothing about poultry raising as a commercial proposition. The long and short of it is that the C.P.R. Company in the person of J. G. Rutherford offered me the job of poultry manager at Strathmore, Alberta, at a salary of $75.00 a month plus a free house, cheap coal, plus a free pass on the railway for myself and my family after a year's service. So it was that in the autumn of the year 1917, my wife, my son and our new daughter moved to Strathmore, a small town of some 500 people located on what was then the main line of the C.P.R. about 30 miles east of Calgary.

715 William Street, London, Ontario.
The house where I was born.

Myself at 18. First year of apprenticeship as a brick mason.

Orpington young stock.
My first experience as a poultry fancier — 1908.

My sister, friend
and self.
London, 1908.

Coughlin Brothers Threshing Crew
Clearwater, Manitoba, 1905.
X = Myself aged 17 years.

*Myself on Elbow River
Mission Bridge, Calgary, 1911.*

*Myself near Prince's Island, Bow River
Calgary, 1911*

In North Hill, Calgary (present-day Rosedale) – 1911.

View from American Hill, Calgary. 1911.
X = Our first home where Harry was born in 1913.

Archie Still and myself, 1912.

My wife , Jane and I, with children Strathmore, 1917.

House and chicken plant, Strathmore, Alberta

Barred Rock Pullets — Strathmore.

"Renfrew" — 1st Prize R.O.P. Cockerel,
"Royal" Toronto, 1925. (Laywell Poultry Farm.)

First meeting of R.O.P. Inspectors, Vancouver, B.C. — 1924. Left to right: Russell
Zavits, "Red" McMurtry, Harry Garrity, Myself, Hugh Greenwood, Ernie Nash.

7

Before saying anything about my management of the poultry department of the Canadian Pacific Railway Company's Demonstration Farm, I think I ought to explain what that farm was, and what part it played in the Company's activities. As most people know the C.P.R. Company owned a great deal of land given to them by the Canadian Government in order to induce investors to provide the money to build a transcontinental railway. All in all the C.P.R. possessed, or had possessed and sold off, something more than 20,000,000 acres of land in western Canada. Land in Alberta where the lines of the C.P.R. ran tended to be dry or semi-desert, and it was the idea of the Company's directors before World War I that irrigation might make some of the land an attractive proposition for families interested in working areas of 40 acres. A big investment was made in building an irrigation system which took water out of Bow River at several points and ran it in big ditches and reservoirs on the north of the course of the river, which ran in a south-easterly direction from Calgary. In order to people the irrigated areas the Company built a Demonstration Farm at Strathmore, the purpose of which was to demonstrate to prospective farmers what could be done on irrigated land and, if the truth be told, to discover what could be done. The C.P.R.'s purpose was to bring in people and sell them land, railway services and water.

Experience showed that there were several flaws in the idea of irrigating this part of Alberta and planting small farmers there—at least at the stage of development which Alberta had reached in 1905 and at any time until 1945. In the first place a family cannot make a decent living on forty acres unless they farm it intensively, and there is no point in farming intensively unless the farmer can sell what he produces. He produces in order to find the money to buy what he cannot produce himself such as manufactured goods of all kinds. Of course, a family can get by on forty acres if they live like hill billies or primitive peasants, but even this is difficult in Alberta east of the foothills because there is insufficient fuel to keep warm enough in winter to survive. And so markets were indispensable for farmers working a small acreage intensively. There were no good markets in Alberta or anywhere close enough to bear the cost of transport. The only things a farmer could raise and sell in Alberta at that time were cereal grains, beef cattle and hogs. This was so, because these commodities could be shipped cheaply enough and produced cheaply enough to sell for cash in the big, populous markets far away from Alberta.

Farmers bought or rented forty-acre farms in the irrigated areas, but they soon jumped over the fence and were working larger areas big enough to yield them the cash necessary to live decently and to live at all. It might be supposed that irrigation would have a place in cereal farming, but this turned out not to be the case—at least not directly. Irrigation laterals broke up fields and made them difficult to harvest with the then existing machines. The water was cold in the spring and this retarded growth. This was serious in a place like Alberta where the growing season is short and freeze-up comes at an uncertain time, and often early. Cereal farmers did, however, learn to flood the low-lying parts of their farms in the autumn and let the water soak in and freeze. This provided insurance against a dry year, and made them reasonably certain of a crop on the low-lying land even if there was insufficient rainfall for an overall good crop.

In the long run I think the Demonstration Farm did demonstrate some things of permanent value. For example the

Farm showed that sunflowers flourished in irrigated land and provide excellent fodder for cattle. We demonstrated, too, that poultry production could be increased. But irrigation and the Demonstration Farm never solved the problem of markets, at least in the way the C.P.R. Company thought they would, and at the time they hoped they would.

Ironically the C.P.R. Company as itself a market, made the Demonstration Farm a viable commercial proposition. Already when I arrived, the Demonstration Farm was being transformed into a supply farm, and in fact the name was changed to the C.P.R. Supply Farm while I was there. The C.P.R. itself was a large consumer of the commodities which are produced on a small acreage: milk, eggs, poultry, butter and cream, honey and meats of various kinds. The C.P.R. operated several large hotels: the Royal Alexandra at Winnipeg; the Palliser at Calgary and others at various main centres. It also operated two large luxury holiday hotels in the mountains: the Banff Springs Hotel and the Chalet Lake Louise. In the days before skiing was a Canadian sport these were open only in the summers. Then there were the dining cars. The dining cars on the C.P.R. were the best restaurants in Canada, and at least half the passengers on the transcontinental trains had to eat in the dining cars or starve, even though they had to pay as much as $2.00 for dinner and $1.25 for breakfast.

And so my job at Strathmore was to supply the hotel, dining cars, work camps, and irrigation maintenance crews with eggs and poultry. Such was the railway's own demand, that I was obliged not only to produce but to buy eggs and poultry from the farmers in an area of 10—12 miles around Strathmore.

When I arrived in October, 1917, the poultry farm was terribly run down. There was a flock of 2,000 birds: half Barred Plymouth Rocks, and half Rhode Island Reds. A large percentage were infected with tuberculosis. My first day I gathered seven eggs. J. G. Rutherford recognized the situation, and he told me he would not expect much for two years.

The capital equipment of the poultry department was, generally speaking, good. The poultry houses were well constructed with lofts insulated with straw. There were the two long laying houses, a large brooder house and a store house of two storeys. There were perhaps a dozen small but well built colony houses where young chickens were raised and allowed to run at large on the range. Along one side of the poultry farm there was an irrigation ditch about seven feet wide and two feet deep, bordered by bushes and willow trees. The land sloped gently away from the ditch towards the valley of a small creek and was bounded by a road which ran parallel to the creek three or four feet below the level of the farm. Thus the whole area of the farm was dry and the meadows were lush on account of the effect of the water soaking into the soil from the irrigation ditches and from the furrows I used to plough through the chicken runs to allow a small flow of irrigation water for the chickens to drink in the spring, summer and autumn.

But there were some unaccountable gaps in the equipment of the farm. There was no permanent water supply: no well and no connection with the piped water supply of the main part of the farm. One of my most tedious and heavy jobs was to haul ten eight gallon cans of water every day from the wells and water tank of the main farm about ¼ of a mile from the poultry plant. This was required by the flock and by my family. Before I left Strathmore in 1923, I connected up the farm with the piped water supply, but I had to do this myself, and had only the resources to put in a single galvanized iron pipe a foot below the surface of the earth, and hence unusable in winter.

The living accommodation for my family consisted of a large two storey house of frame construction. It had a wide verandah running around two sides. There was a large kitchen and pantry, a dining room and a sitting room on the ground floor. Above these were three bedrooms. There was a good basement, and a large hot air furnace for heating the whole house. But there was no bathroom and no water supply. We had to use chamber pots and an outdoor privy. We had to bathe in the kitchen in galvanized iron tubs and wash in enamel bowls. Three eight gallon galvanized steel milk cans with heavy steel lids always stood on the back stoop, or open verandah, in summer and in the kitchen in winter with a dipper hanging above them. There were some electric lights on the ground floor of the house, but the coal fired steam generators on the Farm had ceased to function, and the small gasoline driven lighting plant functioned uncertainly and only when basic needs, which did not include the convenience and comfort of the farm workers, required its use. For all practical purposes we had to rely upon kerosene lamps with tall glass chimneys.

To describe this house is to describe a kind of slavery into which my wife was delivered. Janie had lived in London, where she had been brought up, and in Toronto where she had worked before our marriage. She had always lived in houses with running water and for most of her life with electricity for lighting and other purposes. In Strathmore she was thrown back into another age, much like that which had obtained in America during its first settlement. But she was a hard worker and an ingenious one. To raise four children (for by the time we left Strathmore we had this number) in a house such as I have described meant unremitting work day in and day out. The only time she ever let up was on Sundays, when she limited herself to preparing a Sunday dinner which we ate in the dining room, put on her best clothes, and sometimes went to church and read the *Good Housekeeping* magazine, the *Strathmore Standard,* the *Toronto Saturday Night*, or the *Country Gentleman.*

To describe work in the kitchen of our house on the C.P.R. Farm is sufficient to give some idea of what was involved in being a farm wife fifty years ago. There was no refrigeration. Food was kept cool in the cellar which was reached by lifting a trap door in the pantry, and by descending a flight of stairs into the ill-lit gloom of the basement. The central feature of the kitchen was the range: a large cast iron stove weighing five or six hundred pounds, and made by McLary's Stove Company of London, Ontario. This was fueled by coal or wood in a fire box which held forty to fifty pounds of coal from the Galt mine near Lethbridge, Alberta. Wood was used less often, and mostly for starting the fire. The range heated up completely, and gave a steady warmth. My wife has always maintained that for cooking nothing ever beat a McLary's cast iron range. But it produced a very hot kitchen, desirable enough in the winter, but a hell place in summer. Sometimes in summer we let the range go out, and cooked on a kerosene stove in a shed off the kitchen.

At one end of the range was a reservoir from which hot water could be dipped. Flat irons with removeable spring handles were heated on the flat surface for ironing clothes. Clothes were boiled in an oblong copper boiler on wash day. Wash day which was always a Monday—just as Tuesday was always ironing day—meant much physical labour. Galvanized steel tubs were set out. All cotton clothing and bed linen were soaked in luke warm water. Then each piece was scrubbed with laundry soap in hot water on a scrubbing board made of corrugated metal or glass. Then the cottons were boiled. The next process was rinsing in cold water. Finally the clothes were wrung out using a hand operated wringer with two rollers covered with hard rubber. Then everything was hung out to dry. Woollens, which included in winter the long union suits worn alike by men and women on the farms, were washed separately omitting the boiling process. The scrubbing and rinsing process was reduced somewhat by the purchase of a hand operated washing machine, but the use of this machine meant sessions lasting up to twenty minutes, of turning the tub full of water back and forth by hand. When one considers that the water used in these several processes had to be poured and emptied by hand one can get some idea of the effort involved in keeping a family clean in these circumstances. And we were always clean. Everyone had clean underwear on Sundays, and I always started work on Monday morning in a clean work shirt under my overalls, and I always had a clean shirt on Sundays. Janie never starched my collars. This was done by the Chinaman, Look Hung Lung who ran a laundry in the town.

Then there was the matter of preserving fruit and making pickles. Very little fruit grew in Alberta, but we used to buy raspberries, strawberries, peaches, loganberries, apricots, crab apples and plums by the case. These were brought in generally from British Columbia, but some came from Ontario. As a result of many days of hot, laborious work Janie filled the fruit cupboard in the cellar, so that from September until the next May or June we had bottled fruit three or four times a week.

Apart from work of this description Janie made all the children's outer clothing: suits, trousers, dresses, pinafores—the lot. Underwear was bought from the T. Eaton Company's mail order store in Winnipeg, and so were stockings, overalls, and overcoats and hats.

When one adds to all this the fact that the stores in Strathmore, the church and Memorial Hall, where picture shows were held, were 1 to 1½ miles distant, and the only means of getting there was walking, one gains some idea of what life was like for my wife. Furthermore there was no telephone in the house, although there was one in the brooder house of the poultry farm. I never knew anyone, least of all my wife, ever make a social call on it. It existed solely for business purposes, and, because it was fixed to a wall, one was obliged to stand to use it.

I have already remarked that I knew nothing about poultry farming as an industry when J. G. Rutherford appointed me. This is, if anything, an understatement, because what I did know was based on the assumption that chickens are meant to be beautiful not useful. As a sometime poultry fancier I regarded the laying of eggs as an indispensable part of a chicken's life, not as one of the purposes of its existence as far as human beings are concerned. Now I was in the business I had to learn otherwise. Where to begin with a flock of weak and unproductive chickens?

When I look back on it I now realise that the most valuable thing I found on the C.P.R.'s poultry farm as far as I am concerned personally, was a pile of old poultry magazines and books stored in a cupboard under the stairs in our dwelling house: *The Poultry Review* published in Toronto; and the *Reliable Poultry Journal* published in Quincy, Illinois. There was T.E. Quisenberry's *Producing Poultry Profitably* and a book by a friend of Jack London, Walter Hogan, to which he had given the title: *The Call of the Hen.* These were the beginnings which prompted me to start assembling a small collection of books on poultry. I began to read them night after night by the light of an oil lamp on the kitchen table, my back warmed by the heat of the McLary's range. They opened my eyes to facts and techniques of the poultry industry as it existed in Canada and the United States in 1917.

I began to learn about the poultry business when it was still in its infancy, or at least in its early childhood. Nothing or very little, of what I learned then is still practical today, but what I learned was a stage in the development of the industry to the point where today eggs and poultry are the cheapest and most abundant protein food there is, and everyone takes them for granted. This was not always so. Eggs and poultry produced on the scale they are today, are as much a product of accumulated scientific knowledge, attention to detail and skilful organization as the automobile industry or medical care or any of the other activities of modern society. I was in at the beginning, or if not at the beginning, at least at the Tin Lizzie stage of the business.

The first discovery I made about my new trade was the importance of being able to tell a hen which could lay eggs from one which could not. The art of culling a flock was a basic skill which I had to learn, for upon this skill depended whether one was throwing away feed and wasting space on useless hens, or nourishing and caring for a bird whose eggs paid for its keep and returned a profit to its owner. Culling I learned by reading and doing. Simply put, culling depends on sight and touch: a recognition from the examination of a hen's head of certain characteristics of the comb and eyes; and an examination with the fingers of the hen's pelvic region to determine size, pliability, moisture and skin texture. Of course one's judgment by this method had to be backed up by the test of results: did the hen one thought would lay eggs actually do so. This test could be made by counting and averaging the production of a determined group confined together in a house and pen before and after culling. Better still one could identify each hen by a numbered metal or celluloid band on one of its legs, and then trap nest it, i.e. let it lay its eggs in a nest from which it could not be released except by the person wishing to record its performance of the art of laying an egg. By this means I was able to test my skill at judging hens which could or could not lay eggs. The layers I kept; the others were sold off or killed for their flesh.

One essential item of equipment missing in the poultry department of the C.P.R. Farm was trap nests. Because the C.P.R. Company was unwilling to invest anything further I was obliged to convert my labour into their capital. I bought a single example of a commercially produced trap nest manufactured by the Morgan Company of London, Ontario. Using this as a model I built 100 trap nests. In this case the skill in rough carpentry I had learned in the building business stood me in good stead.

At this time in Canada it was estimated by the statisticians of the government that hens kept on commercial poultry farms laid an average of 80 eggs a year. Nowadays one normally expects a hen bred for eggs to lay at least 300 or more eggs a year. Culling alone has not produced this increase in productivity. In fact culling is no longer a necessary skill. Progress towards high productivity has been primarily a matter of breeding. While profitable management of a flock depended in those days on eliminating the poor layers, culling them out by itself could not produce high layers. This depended on breeding. Study in agricultural colleges in Canada and the United States led to the conclusion that the ability of a hen to lay eggs was a physical characteristic transmitted genetically through the males. If one could identify and segregate the sons of high laying hens and exclusively use them as breeders, then it would follow that high laying strains could be developed and the average number of high laying hens would increase from generation to generation.

Just before World War I the son of a farmer in the Ottawa Valley, W. A. Brown, who had studied in the agricultural college of the state of Maine, devised a plan for improving egg production in Canada through state action based upon this notion that high laying characteristics in hens are transmitted through the male. W.A. Brown persuaded the Canadian Department of Agriculture that there ought to be set up by the department a system of recording the performance of hens, and issuing certificates of performance which would enable the owners of the hens to sell the fertile eggs of these hens for hatching purposes or the males hatched from their eggs for breeding purposes.

When World War I ended W. A. Brown's scheme was inaugurated, and was known throughout the poultry industry as R.O.P., Record of Performance. The scheme was voluntary. In 1920 I entered a flock of Barred Plymouth Rocks and a flock of Rhode Island Reds in the R.O.P. My flock was one of the earliest entries in Western Canada.

The scheme worked like this. The owner, in this case the C.P.R. Company, paid a fee of $15.00 for a flock of 50 birds, and a reducing fee for larger numbers. The owner then undertook to abide by the rules of the scheme and to admit an inspector to check on his or her observation of the rules. The first rule was that the R.O.P. flock be segregated from all other birds on the farm. The chickens were required to be of a recognized pure breed. The R.O.P. flock had to be trap nested, and the production of each individual hen recorded on forms supplied by the government. Each hen had to be individually identified by a metal leg band bearing a unique number sealed on the hen's leg with a tiny led slug on which a crown was imprinted by the punch used to close the seal. This was done by a government inspector when he passed the hen for entry. The flock was entered for a calendar year, and at the end of the year the production of each bird individually could be calculated from the record sheets: one for each month. Any hen which had laid 150 eggs in the year was assigned a certificate, and any fertile eggs laid by her or any males hatched from eggs laid by her could be sold as certified stock of a high laying strain. Of course the fertile eggs or male progeny of hens laying 200 or more eggs commanded premium prices. In this way the comparatively few poultry breeders willing to take the trouble of entering flocks in R.O.P. were able at a profit to themselves to diffuse high laying strains among the poultry population as a whole, and to enable farmers who wanted to increase their egg production to buy stock which had some chance of high production.

Of course much more is known today about the genetic transmission of the capacities and characteristics of poultry. As a result the breeding practices of the 1920's and 1930's have long since been superseded. Today a three way cross produces birds with desired characteristics or combinations of characteristics, but the birds having the desired characteristics such as a capacity to lay eggs or to become well fleshed are the end of the line. They have only ancestors, not descendants.

In learning to cull a flock and to understand breeding I mastered what were then the essentials of the poultryman's trade, but there was, as there still is, much more to the business than the essentials. The incubating of fertile eggs was at that time more an art than a science. In order to increase production one could not rely on the whole process of nature. Hens are clever in the matter of hatching their chicks, but they are unproductive while doing so, and there are too many hazards involved in letting hens brood their own chicks. In order to overcome the deficiencies of nature, poultrymen have been obliged to learn from hens and do better than they. When I began to learn about incubation, men and machines were doing only slightly better than hens.

Basically an incubator is a machine by the use of which the operator seeks to duplicate the work which a hen does in warming eggs with her body in order to hatch them. Heat is introduced into the machine. There is first the problem of controlling the temperature: easy today when electricity is used and thermostatic devices exist, but not so easy when the heat source was kerosene, or coal fires. The eggs have to be turned over during the hatching period and cooled for certain periods of time. A hen does this very skilfully, and so do modern incubators, but fifty years ago the cooling and turning of eggs was a tedious and exacting job, requiring precise timing, patience and also speed of manipulation.

The poultry department of the C.P.R. Farm possessed the most up-to-date incubator of the pre—1914 period: very large by the standards of the day, and capable of incubating six hundred eggs at a time in each unit. They were manufactured by the Candee Company of Pennsylvania. There were also a few small kerosene-heated incubators. An indispensable complement of incubators were brooders, which can best be described as heated tents, which served as substitutes for the mother hen until the chicks were old enough to produce bodily warmth sufficient for individual survival. As in the case of incubation, so in the process of brooding, electricity has simplified everything and made things more exact and manageable. Not so in the 1920's. Brooders heated with kerosene or other combustible materials required close, individual attention.

Given the kind of equipment I had for incubation and the brooding of chicks it is easy to see why there was much personal skill, adaptability and hard exacting labour required to achieve any worthwhile result. From early January, when the hatching started, until mid-September, when the new gener-

106

ation of chickens were fully feathered and some ready to produce, I was obliged to work 18 hours a day, six days a week, and a mere 12 hours on Sunday, the day of rest.

One of the problems with the kind of incubators I had was the regulation of the draughts on the coke-fired heating plant. Strathmore is only about 110 miles from the first range of the Rocky Mountains, and the winds were often strong and variable. In order to overcome the effect of the wind on the flow of smoke up the chimneys I got Tommy Moran, the town tinsmith, and brother of the famous professional hockey player, Amby Moran, to build out of galvanized sheeting 15-foot extensions to the chimneys. When sober, Tommy was a good craftsman, but even his handiwork did not entirely solve the problem of stabilizing the daughts of the heating system, and I developed an old time sailor's sensitivity to changes in the wind. I could even feel a change of the wind in my sleep, and more than once I rushed from my bed at three or four in the morning to see that the fires were under control.

Another problem of incubation related to obtaining and stabilizing the right degree of humidity in the incubators. The Candee incubators were built in Pensylvania and the directions for their use assumed conditions such as existed on the Central Atlantic seaboard of the United States. It took me a while to cotton on to the fact that the incubators had to be altered in their operation to take account of the high, dry atmosphere of western Alberta, and that additional moisture had to be introduced into the machines. This I effected by altering their ventilation and by the installation of a kind of humidifier depending on wet flannel.

A poultryman is concerned not only with producing eggs but with insuring their keeping qualities. The preservation of the freshness of an egg does not depend alone on refrigeration and the rapidity of marketing. Keeping qualities start with the hen herself. When I started in the business, serious commercial poultrymen no longer believed in the rural lore to the effect that hens did not lay eggs unless roosters ran with the hens and had sexual intercourse with them. Laying eggs and their fertilization are separate physiological processes, which family planners of all kinds seek to keep separate. In the case of poultry planners the object of keeping hens separate from males, except for breeding purposes, is to improve the keeping qualities of the eggs. Fertile eggs deteriorate and go bad faster than infertile ones, and furthermore infertile eggs are less likely to contain blood spots and meat spots which render eggs objectionable and liable to quick spoilage.

In order to increase the possibility of the consumer's purchasing a fresh, useable egg, the first process after gathering the eggs is candling. This is the inspection of each egg with the assistance of a beam of light in order to determine its age by the size of the air pocket at one end, whether it is fertile or infertile and the presence or absence of spots in the yolk or cracks in the shell. Candling is now automatized, but until very recently candling was a skilled job requiring concentration of attention, trained eyesight and dexterity and speed with the fingers in handling the eggs. On the whole women were better at this job than men for the same reason that they are generally better than men at fine sewing, knitting and similar work.

The killing of poultry is a skilled job, one which is still with us and one which still requires the same personal understanding and dexterity as it always has done. In the commercial poultry business all birds are killed. A chicken which dies of disease, accident or old age is a dead loss to the business. It follows that the vast majority of poultry have their lives ended by a human being just as they have their lives started by the same agency. To discuss the killing of poultry usually generates disgust. In my view this is hypocrisy unless one is a vegetarian. Every man or woman who eats the flesh of a living creature participates in its death. It is moral nonsense to object to knowing how animals die so that men may live, and to hold in contempt those who kill them.

A poultry killer employs an extremely sharp, fine-pointed knife. He must know where to make two cuts and how to make them quickly and surely. The object of the one cut is to sever the main artery in the throat. The object of the other is to sever the main nerves in the brain. The first cut insures the quick discharge of the blood from the carcass; the second the total relaxation of the bird's nervous system so that the feathers are removed with little effort. Both together insure instantaneous death. I have never detected in poultry the presentiment of death which is observed among cattle in slaughterhouses.

In the successful raising of poultry feeding, watering and cleanliness are of the utmost importance. In my time the individual poultryman had to use his own experience and judgment in these matters, but, as in much else, increased productivity depended on following the findings of the scientists in agricultural colleges. I always found that the practice recommended by scientists on the basis of their observations and discoveries paid off, if applied in the light of experience and with a common sense regard for one's immediate circumstances. One had always to be aware that findings about birds and animals in one part of the country were not always true in other parts. That is why two or three agricultural colleges or research stations are, or should be, maintained in each region of Canada.

One part of the poultry business about which I learned very little in Strathmore, was the marketing and financial side. I was strictly a production man, and that is why I never grew rich out of the business. I never had to learn anything about selling or financing my operations. The C.P.R. provided a market which was undersupplied by the C.P.R.'s own farm. I learned something about buying inasmuch as I bought eggs and poultry which I processed and shipped to the C.P.R. hotels and dining cars, and I did sell day-old baby chicks and breeding stock, but this was incidental to my main work. I learned nothing about accounting or pricing. The railway officials fixed the price at which the produce of the farm was credited in the Company's books, and supplies such as feed, equipment and stock were debited at the prices paid. This was all handled by Les Campbell, the accountant for the whole Supply Farm. I never knew how much money I was making for the C.P.R. except that in six years they doubled my salary and gave me small bonuses from time to time. They even gave me a bus man's holiday which enabled me to visit some of the big poultry farms in Ontario, like that of John S. Martin at Port Dover, the Ontario Agricultural College at Guelph, and MacDonald College at St. Anne de Belleville near Montreal. An indication of how intensely interested in my job I was is the fact that although I was near Montreal when I visited MacDonald College I never thought of visiting the largest city in Canada, reputed to be the wickedest, richest and most lively place in the country, and the headquarters of the C.P.R.

About financing I learned nothing. If I had, I think I could have overcome the fright I experienced when my contracting business failed. If I had learned something about financing a business I could have gone into poultry farming on my own, and got for myself what I earned for the C.P.R., or I could have gone into the hatching business. This is now a very big business, but it was then in its infancy. After all, I had developed for the C.P.R. one of the first commercial hatchery businesses in western Canada. I could have done the same for myself, had I had the knowledge and self confidence to find financial backing. But I did not.

Poultry production as I learned the business in Strathmore, Alberta, was then in a rather primitive stage of development from being a farmyard activity relying on lore and the simple processes of nature to being what it is today, an industrialized and scientific activity. Most of the hard physical labour and personal skill based on sight, sound, touch and accumulated experience and feeling have gone out of the business, and have been replaced by techniques of observation, measurement and mechanized manipulation and control. I think it is still the case, that a successful poultry business like any business having to do with living creatures, animal or vegetable, requires in it men and women who are focal points of knowledge, understanding, responsibility and feeling about what they are doing and the creatures they are using. Canada, I think, is fortunate in having somehow preserved something of this spirit of personal interest, and that is probably why Canada is still a large food producer at a time when many nations have abandoned the virtues of farmyard production without establishing anything successful to put in its place.

8

Whenever I read *Sunshine Sketches of a Little Town* I wish that Stephen Leacock could have lived for a time in Strathmore, Alberta. I am sure he could have put down on paper what that town was like. Another man of a different kind, Sinclair Lewis, could have done this, too. But to the best of my knowledge nobody has.

Prairie towns in western Canada are not generally speaking very attractive to look at. Strathmore, Alberta, was an exception. I think this was due mainly to the trees. Because the C.P.R. wanted to persuade people to buy land in this part of Alberta, they had put some real effort into making Strathmore different and attractive. Part of this effort consisted in planting trees and making a park with a little lake in it. The lake had been an ordinary prairie slough, but the engineers of the Irrigation Department had cleaned it up and raised the water level by means of a small earth dam. Trees had been planted, and by the time we came to live in Strathmore the trees, mainly fast growing poplars with a scatter of conifers and Manitoba maples, were a fair size. The prairie grass was cut a few times a year. The result was that Strathmore possessed something which very few little towns had fifty years ago. Some wooden sheds had been put up on the shore of the lake so that people could change into swimming suits, and there were some diving boards and platforms where swimmers could hoist themselves out of the water and lie in the sun. When the C.P.R. lost interest in Strathmore as a show place, the town people paid no attention to their park. The lake was never cleaned out periodically and the whole thing reverted to the wilderness.

In addition to the park there were other groves of trees in and around Strathmore. The Demonstration Farm itself was well treed, and the premises of the Irrigation Department—the I.D. as we always called it—was beautifully treed. The homes of the I.D. engineers and workmen and their store houses and equipment sheds seemed almost to be set in a forest of a kind hard to find on the prairies. In a sense the trees were a demonstration of what irrigation water could do to a semi-desert with a low rainfall, for it was the water which enabled the trees to grow sufficiently big and strong to withstand the hail storms, which could strip the bark as well as the leaves off ill-nourished trees and so kill them.

Apart from the park and the trees Strathmore was a pretty average prairie town: a main street lined with square fronted two storey stores of frame construction. There were not more than a half dozen structures of brick: the Bank of Montreal was one. Main Street straggled off and lost itself in the prairie. Streets branched off Main Street. Some were dirt trails, but some had wooden sidewalks. There was a wooden sidewalk, maybe half a mile in length which ran from the Empress Hotel on the corner of Main Street to the school and beyond to the I.D. It ran parallel to the perimeter of the park. Along this street were a livery stable and blacksmith shop, a garage and a number of dwelling houses up to a point about 500 yards from the school. If one walked from the Empress Hotel to the point where the dwelling houses ceased one came on open prairie stretching far away to the right, and then there was the school yard.

Strathmore was better supplied with schools than most prairie towns. There was a four-room public school of two storeys and of frame construction. It was built over a large basement six or eight feet above ground level. In the same yard was a High School, the second storey of which was finished in cedar shingles. The school yard was fenced with wire, and at the back of the school yard there was the house of the school janitor, and along one side a line of privies. Education given in these schools suffered from the same defects which afflicted most rural schools: the turn-over of staff. Few people wanted to make a career of teaching in country towns. The School Boards in Calgary, Edmonton, and the bigger towns like Lethbridge paid more than rural schools, and living in the cities was more attractive than living in the country. The result was that the rural schools tended to be staffed by newcomers or by people who could not secure appointments in the cities. Two of our children attended Strathmore School, and they seemed to have made a reasonable start, but when they entered Stanley Jones School in Calgary it was assumed, until proved to the contrary, that they would be about a year behind the city children in achievement. It should be stated that at least one boy, the son of a grocer, who went through school in Strathmore became a Rhodes Scholar and went to Oxford University, and my own eldest son graduated with a distinguished first class from Cambridge University.

Apart from the C.P.R. operation there, Strathmore was like any other prairie town in its purposes: a stopping point on the railway where farmers shipped their produce to the markets of the world, where they bought supplies shipped in from elsewhere in Canada; where they banked their money and obtained credit; and where they amused themselves when they could find the time. The eye could discern what Strathmore was. In most villages in Europe, the biggest structure one can see is a church. Even in the small towns of Ontario and Quebec churches are usually the largest buildings, and sometimes factories. In Strathmore, as in all prairie towns the biggest structures by far were the grain elevators. They dominated the skyline: one clad in metal sheeting which glistened in the sun: one painted a dark red-brown and the other white. Because there were a few ranches in the area Strathmore had a small stock yard where cattle destined for the slaughter house in Calgary were loaded on cattle cars.

In those days the town was almost entirely dependent on the railway. Every day the eastbound and westbound transcontinental trains stopped at the Strathmore station discharging and taking aboard passengers, and goods shipped in the baggage cars, the mail and newspapers and magazines. The transcontinental line ran through Strathmore then, and continued to do so until a new line was built which avoided the marshy ground at Eagle Lake, east of Strathmore. Twice a week the way freight trains stopped in Strathmore and spent several hours shunting freight cars on to the sidings and picking up loaded ones or empties as the case might be. Each day the Trans Canada Limited sped through Strathmore without stopping, but Strathmore was a flag stop for the Trans Canada. If it ever did stop to take on or discharge a passenger there was much speculation in the town as to who was important enough to ride the Trans Canada.

Townspeople congregated at the station daily—sometimes to meet people or pick up parcels and perishable products sent by express in the baggage cars—but also just out of curiosity and from the attraction of seeing a great train and its crew: the engineer looking down from his cab in a blue and white striped overall, wearing a blue and white striped peaked cap with a puffy crown; and the fireman with a kerchief around his neck; the conductor and trainsmen in smooth dark blue serge with gold on their caps; and the baggage men and mail clerks exchanging a few words from the great sliding doors; sleeping car porters who were always black men in clean white jackets and dark trousers; and the cooks and waiters in the dining car; and sometimes the passengers sitting at the snowy-white linen-covered tables, eating. But this last was not often seen because the Transcontinental stopped in Strathmore about 4 p.m. one way, and about 2:30 p.m. the other. There was always the dramatic moment when all were aboard except the conductor. He held his watch in his hand, and as the exact second arrived he signalled the engineer to start. The whistle was blown in recognition of the signal, and the train began to move; the conductor looked for the trainman's signal from the rear, and then swung himself on to the step of a car, and one could see the trainmen and the sleeping-car porters slamming down the iron platforms and closing the doors as the great train gathered momentum past the distance signal at green.

The C.P.R. Company also provided a means of quick communication by telegraph. The station agent and his assistant were both telegraph operators. One of them always sat in front of a telegraph instrument, in a sort of bay window jutting a few feet out of the line of the station. The telegraph instrument was heard chattering almost continuously. The operator sat in a round-backed wooden chair with two thin steel rods holding the back firmly to the seat. It was the usual practice of the operators to put porcelain or glass insulators from the telegraph lines on to the legs of their chairs so that they could be pushed more easily over the wooden floors. The operator almost always wore a green celluloid eye shade. People marvelled at the ability of the operator sitting casually with his feet on the desk reading the *Calgary Herald* or the *Albertan* to recognize amid the chattering of the telegraph the signal for Strathmore to start receiving, when he hastily put down his paper, grabbed a pencil and began writing on a yellow pad. Most often the message had to do with the working of the railway. When a message was typed and put in an envelope, people began to wonder who had lost a relative somewhere. Somehow, telegrams were associated with news of death.

Fifty years ago people did not travel much by automobile, and there were still very few about. Most were model T Fords. Some people did go as far as Calgary by car, but this could be a troublesome journey over dusty and sometimes muddy roads. But I owe my life to being able to travel by car to Calgary. This occurred when one day I nicked myself with a killing knife. In spite of cleansing the wound, my arm began to redden, and the doctor told me there was nothing for it but to go to Calgary for treatment. The trains had gone. I was driven to Calgary in a little more than an hour, and arrived in time to avoid disaster.

It must not be supposed that meeting the trains was the only diversion in Strathmore. As to amusements Strathmore provided as much as could be found in most towns. There was a baseball park with a few wooden stands for spectators. On Wednesday evenings and on Saturdays and Sundays during summer the Strathmore team played teams from other towns like Gleichen, Rockyford, Bassano and Cheadle. In winter there was skating and hockey on a rink made by flooding a piece of land. The rink was illuminated by electric lights strung on wires about 12 feet or so above the ice. There was also a curling rink which was roofed in.

Strathmore was visited from time to time by a small travelling circus with side shows, a ferris wheel and merry-go-round. Then there was the Chautauqua. This was a travelling group which pitched its tent and provided more elevated and educational entertainment: illustrated talks on distant places, music and the non-partisan discussion of public issues. In 1921 the townspeople built a Memorial Hall, where there were dances and where movies were shown usually one afternoon and one evening a week.

As I remember it there were three churches in Strathmore: the Methodist Church, which was the largest, St. Michael and All Angels, which was Anglican, and a small Roman Catholic Church, which probably bore the name of a saint, but was always referred to simply as "the Catholic Church". All these were of frame construction, and were painted white. We were members of the Anglican Church, and our children went to Sunday School there. The minister (all Protestant clergy were called ministers) for most of our time in Strathmore was the Rev. A. W. Currie, an underfed Scotsman. He was not an impressive man, but he was a kind man and a good one. He was worth having in Strathmore because he seemed to be more gentle and less self-seeking than the average. He used to walk enormous distances visiting his scattered flock. I can remember very well the time he was caught in a terrible hail storm and arrived at our house dripping and battered after having to shelter from the hail under some bushes. He was his own verger and bell ringer, and he was obliged to look after the church's heating system, a large furnace which delivered hot air in a single great wave from an iron grill in the floor in front of the altar rail. On one cold day he had had trouble with the furnace, and the service started late. When finally he raised his hand to give the blessing, the congregation could see the palm: black as the ace of spades. On the way out one of his parishioners, Mrs. Glendenning, the mother of a numerous family, all twins, was heard to say in her broad Scots accent, "Ah, puir Currie, no one will ever know what he has to endure."

The majority of the people in and around Strathmore were Anglo-Saxons, but not all were Canadians by birth. There were a large number of Americans in this part of Alberta, and indeed in every part of the province. In Alberta in the 1920's there were still large tracts of land open to homesteading, and I, myself had sometimes thought of trying my luck in the Peace River country. For many years I had on my bookshelf a monograph on the Peace River published by the Canadian Department of Lands and Immigration giving figures about rainfall, reports on soil, growing seasons and so on. Since 1900 or earlier, American farmers had been coming into Alberta in search of new land, and it is not therefore surprising that a substantial number of the people in the district were Anglo-Saxons in descent but were not Canadians. This had some effect upon the character of the community. My eldest son once told me that the first political argument he ever had was in the school yard in Strathmore when he was seven or eight years old. This was with a boy whose parents came from the U.S.A. The substance of the argument was whether it was better for a country to have a President or a King. As my son remembers it the American kid advanced the proposition that anybody can be President whereas anybody cannot be King. This is probably what is wrong with the United States.

Immigrants from central and eastern Europe were not much in evidence in western Alberta in the early 1920's. There were, however, a few Scandinavians, Dutchmen and Germans in the district. A Dutchman was the manager of the Bank of Montreal. This was the top as far as social ranking went. Curiously the man at the bottom of the heap in Strathmore was also a Dutchman: poor old Bill van Hoeff. He was a labouring man and a drunk. One day he was found dead in his shack, and there was no money to bury him. He was dumped into a rough wooden box and buried on the edge of the cemetery with no ceremony of any kind. Somehow his family in Holland heard of this, and being rather well-to-do, arranged for him to be reburied decently by the Catholic priest. ·

The bakery in Strathmore was run by a big, glum German named Emil Frohburger. Nobody bothered him during the war, but on the day of the Armistice in November, 1918, a delegation of patriots waited on him and forced him to ring the bell in the fire station for a few hours as part of the victory celebrations.

Chinese were more numerous than Germans. One with the family name of Look or Luk ran a hand laundry, and he had three sons: Look Duck Wee, Look Jun and Look Hung Lung. The first two were very bright in school and had remarkable talents for drawing in pencil and in water colours. Another Chinese ran a restaurant. Almost the only servant employed by anyone in Strathmore was a Chinese who worked for an unmarried civil engineer. Some of the women of Strathmore alleged that this servant used to wash the dishes and the kitchen floor with the same cloth, but one could not tell whether this libel was directed at him because he was a man employed in in what seemed to them an unnatural occupation or because he was Chinese.

The only French Canadians in Strathmore were the Giroux family. Old Man Giroux, as he was universally known, was the

119

father of a very large family; 10 or12 children. He was the section foreman of the C.P.R. His job was to look after the right of way, i.e. the tracks, switches and signalling equipment of the railway in Strathmore and for several miles each side of the town. In looking over the track and moving to and fro on his job he used a jigger. This was a small vehicle mounted on flanged wheels which fitted the railway track. It was driven by a gasoline engine, and could seat four men, perched two each side on a piece of wood fastened to the top of the frame. Their feet rested on a kind of running board. The section gang also used a hand-operated car which two men pumped. This vehicle is probably known to everyone on account of the frequency with which Charlie Chaplin, Buster Keaton and the Keystone Cops used such a means of escape from pursuing railway locomotives in films, now shown on T.V.

Half of Old Man Giroux's family were grown up and had left home, except for one son who worked with his father in the section gang. The part of the family which made its mark on Strathmore were the younger boys and the last of the lot, a girl named Germaine, who started school about the same time as our elder son. The younger boys were known only by their nicknames; and around 1920–21 they ranged in age from 9 to 16. They were Teeter and Pie and Chuck and Zeb. Three of them were slow at school, but they were all good athletes. Neither the Strathmore hockey team nor the baseball team could do without Teeter and Pie. Chuck and Zeb showed the makings of good hockey players, and even when he was only 11 or 12 years old Chuck used to catch for the pitchers of the Strathmore baseball team when they were warming up before a game.

There were probably more educated people in Strathmore than in most prairie towns. To the usual doctor or doctors, lawyer, druggist, clergyman and bank manager there was added in Strathmore the engineers of the Irrigation Department and the manager of the C.P.R. farm. These were usually college graduates. But the top people of the C.P.R. operation in Strathmore tended to keep to themselves, just as they lived apart in their own grove of trees. One woman, who was married to an engineer, was what one might call a gentlewoman. She had ideas of conduct and living which were above the level of the town and these were not snobbery on her part. She had very agreeable manners and she never gossiped.

The employees of the C.P.R. Farm hardly formed a group of their own. Most of us were too busy, and if we had any spare time, too tired to have much of a social life. The idea of eating, drinking and playing cards together was almost unknown, but we managed to be friends. The man who ran the creamery was a pleasant, clean little fellow named Kirkland. His wife was related to Senator Michener, and was thus related to Roland Michener, the immediately past Governor General of Canada.

Then there was Mrs. Platt and her husband Henry. Some time before World War I Mrs. Platt emigrated from Southport, Lancashire, in England with her sister Miss Taylor. Somehow these two women ended up in Strathmore, where one of them married an American, Henry Platt, who looked after the C.P.R.'s registered herd of Holstein cattle. Henry was a very silent man, but Mrs. Platt had enough words for both. When we knew her she was a plump little woman with wispy, yellowish hair. She never lost a marked Lancashire accent. In this rich accent she could tell you all you needed to know about Strathmore, and always in a cheerful, half humorous way without malice or ill feeling. In 1963 my elder son and three of my grandsons and I travelled to Calgary by car, and we stopped off to look around Strathmore. We visited the Platts, then well past 80 years of age. Because my grandsons had by then spent 14 years in Britain, Mrs. Platt was interested to hear what young people had to say about the "old country". When the conversation drew to a close, she said, raising her arms in a characteristic gesture, "Ee, and to think I left a nice place like Southport to live in Strathmore," and she chuckled at the joke of it all. Soon after this visit she died.

The management of the C.P.R. Farm was a big, responsible job. The C.P.R. offered as one inducement to take the post, a large, well built and well appointed house. It overlooked the main road out of Strathmore to the east, and in those days it was set well back from the road, in a fine lawn with a huge lilac tree near the front entrance. Today the Trans-Canada Highway has cut off part of the lawn, and the setting is now anything but attractive. Setting or not the house seemed unable to attract a permanent tenant. Instability at the top plagued the Farm during my time, because the turn-over in management was much worse than the turn-over in staff. The manager when I arrived in 1917 was A. D. Campbell. A.D. was a good scout, but he moved on within a short time. He was succeeded by a man named Bertie Auld. Auld was related to one of the high officials of the Canadian Department of Agriculture, and he had a degree from an agricultural college. He seems to have been more attracted by the picturesque aspects of rural life than by its challenge to ingenuity and skill. His eldest son commandeered the use of Hector, the best saddle horse on the farm, a spirited and handsome creature. He used to ride about the farm and "over to town "on Hector in a costume which was a cross between that of a polo player and a cowboy: shiny low brown riding boots and fawn jodphurs on the lower half of him, and a tweed jacket, a colourful shirt with coloured kerchief around his neck, and on his head a ten gallon Stetson hat.

He had other sons, who also rode horses about the place. Whether the sons established in his mind that he was a tribal patriarch is hard to say, but when, either he grew disillusioned with the C.P.R. or the C.P.R. with him, he decided to lead an expedition to Spokane, Washington, in the U.S.A. where it was believed things were marvellous and prosperity assured. Several of the working people on the Farm including Mrs. Platt and her husband Henry, were infected with this enthusiasm, and under Auld's leadership they all departed. I never learned what happened to Auld. He probably ended up in California, but the Platts returned to Strathmore, where Henry was obliged to find a labouring job in the section gang run by Old Man Giroux. His job had been taken by an unmarried man who was even more silent than he and so devoted to his job that he slept in the barn with the cows.

Auld was succeeded for a short time by an uneducated man named Breen, who had been a C.P.R. foreman in some branch of its business. He loudly announced when he moved into the manager's house that he only had a "rocking chair and a mop". Being thus unencumbered with worldly goods it was no trouble for him to move. His successor was the last manager the Farm ever had in my experience, George Jones. He was a youngish man of about my own age, and a college graduate. He abandoned the notion that the farm was for purposes of demonstrating anything, and under him the name was changed to C.P.R. Supply Farm. He did as good a job as was possible given the fact that the Company was unwilling to put any more capital into the enterprise. When the depression came in 1929, George took on the job of managing farms for a mortgage company which was obliged to put in their own man to oversee the working of farms whose owners could no longer pay their mortgages on account of the collapse of prices. The last I heard of him he was doing a good job under the Prairie Farm Rehabilitation Act. George Jones' departure was the beginning of the end of the C.P.R. Farm. The Company eventually sold the irrigation works to a Farmers' Cooperative, sold the Farm for what they could get, and relied on the market for supplies for their dining cars and hotels.

If the Aulds ended up in California it was a destiny which many people around Strathmore hankered after. California was a kind of promised land to some people. One man got there by a combination of calculation and luck as a result of a hail insurance deal. As is well known hail storms are a real hazard of farming on the prairies, especially in western Alberta. But hail is a funny phenomenon. It does not fall uniformly over a wide area, but seems to hit some spots pretty regularly and not others, and for some reason one field can be hailed out and another not touched. The explanation probably has something to do with land formation, the presence of sloughs and so on, which may affect the clouds. Be that as it may, this man discovered this probability that hail would fall here and not there, and he rented a half section where the probability was high. He put in a crop at the least possible cost, insured it to the maximum and waited. Sure enough, there was a great hail storm when the crop was about three inches out of the ground. The insurance company's assessor awarded him 40% of loss on his crop. About six weeks later there was another heavy hail storm. The assessor awarded another 40%. Then came this man's luck. The weather turned hot, the autumn lasted unusually long, and the frost held off until late September. He threshed a crop of 35–40 bushels of oats to the acre. He pocketed the proceeds and went to Calafornia.

The C.P.R. people and the Strathmore people were in some senses separate communities. The important people in the town were merchants, agents of farm machinery companies and the like. I never had many dealings with them because most of the purchases made for my work went through the C.P.R. and my produce, except day-old-chicks and breeding stock, was disposed of in the same way. I knew the butcher, grocers and hardware dealers as a consumer. We were obliged to buy grocery staples and especially meat and fish locally.

The C.P.R. Farm may have been a supply farm, but the only food we ever bought from the farm was milk and butter. everything else came from the local merchants. This was a costly business, because the grocers not only sought to maximize their profits but in order to do business they were obliged, or thought they were obliged, to give a long line of credit to the farmers. Some farmers only paid when they had a good crop, i.e. about every second year. The butchers did less business with the farmers and so were less dependent on them and less of their resources were tied up in this way.

There was a good deal of pushing and hauling in the local business community and competition and new methods intruded from time to time. For example, an Englishman named George Fox bought out Gatenby & Fisher, the principal grocery and general store. Fox introduced the policy of cash sales only, and he reduced prices very markedly. He also fired the principal short-change artist who had flourished for years as a clerk employed by Gatenby & Fisher. You had to count your money when you did business with this fellow, and when one caught him out, he always offered as an excuse the confusion he said was caused to him by the different colours of the notes. In those days only one dollar and two dollar bills were issued by the Canadian Government Treasury. Notes for $5.00, $10.00 etc. were issued by the chartered banks, and they did differ widely in appearance if not in size. But the excuse was no good, and everybody knew it.

Fox reduced prices, did a big business and retired eventually to Bournemouth, England. But cash selling did not reduce competition. We dealt generally with a wholesale house in Calgary which made even better prices to farmers, and we bought a lot of staples like sugar, jam, prunes, peanut butter and so on from this firm. Another way of emancipating oneself from the grip of the local merchants was to deal with the T. Eaton Co's mail order division. Timothy Eaton is the man who prevented consumer cooperatives from flourishing in Canada in the way that producer cooperatives did. T. Eaton's could not be beaten as to prices of every kind of consumer goods, and they ensured quality or money back and no questions asked. In their best days, and these lasted a long time, there was never a more honest and reliable and worthwhile mercantile enterprise than the T. Eaton Co. No one today can appreciate what this firm meant to farmers of western Canada when they had a great deal to put up with from banks, grain dealers, mortgage companies, the hazards of nature and high tariffs.

Strathmore was close to the cattle country, but strangely enough the fish available in the town was better than the meat.

Fish came packed in ice from British Columbia, twice a week on the Transcontinental train. As a result the people of Strathmore ate first quality sockeye salmon more often than they ate good quality beefsteak. The fact is that the butchers of Strathmore got the beasts for slaughter which were not worth sending to the packing houses in Calgary. There was plenty of beef, but one needed good teeth. Sheep breeding was not much developed in Alberta at that time, and lamb and mutton were more or less delicacies. Like the poultry industry the hog industry was still in its infancy. The enterprising and thrifty farmer might keep a few hogs for his own use and he might sell a few for local consumption, but commercial hog breeding was hardly known in and around Strathmore. It is nonsense to suppose that the prairie farmer in the 1920's or at any time, enjoyed an abundance of food grown by himself on his own place, and that the little towns shared this bounty. The farmers only had abundance if they had enough money from cash crops which they could spend on commodities produced commercially elsewhere in Canada and the world: fruit, for example, which did not and could not be grown on the prairies, or woollen clothing which was not produced in western Canada at that time. The list of things indispensable to any reasonable life, which were not or could not be produced on the prairies is a long one. To live half decently (and that is how most farmers lived—only half decently) a farmer had to produce what he could sell to the best advantage and as much of it as he possibly could.

Competition or no competition the merchants of Strathmore did not starve or go bankrupt in the 1920's. George Berry, who kept the hardware store, was the first man in Strathmore to own "a big car". This was a cherry red Chalmers, which conferred upon its owner tremendous prestige. About the peak in automobile ownership in those days was a Dodge Touring car. Dr. Girvin had a Dodge. I do not think anyone in Strathmore rose to the heights of a McLaughlin-Buick, or a Studebaker Super Six. No merchant was that rich, or if there was one, he kept it to himself.

Of the character of these people of importance I did not learn very much. By 1922 I was a well-established man in the C.P.R. and I handled a lot of goods on the Company's behalf. I was asked to join the Masonic Lodge. Masonry depends a lot on ritual, and it was pretty hard to develop much ritual in a room above a store in Strathmore where the only furniture was kitchen chairs bought from Eaton's for 90 cents a piece. I studied the subject, and I was very impressed by the Junior Warden's address to the candidate seeking admission to the Order. But some of the leading figures in the Lodge put me off. They were adulterers and thieves in spite of their Masonic professions. The adultery I learned about after entering the Lodge, and the thieving I learned about after I left Strathmore when some of them were prosecuted for thefts of lumber, building materials and such like from the stores of the C.P.R. Sometimes I have asked myself whether I was asked to join because I handled large quantities of C.P.R. property. As it was, I used to wonder why so many eggs were ordered for Irrigation crews. They seemed to be eating a lot more eggs than anybody I knew.

There were a few flappers about Strathmore. This was a term applied to young women who followed the fashions to extremes, and were believed to live by looser standards than the average. Two girls who worked in the telephone exchange were flappers, and were considered fair game for travelling men. In those days people talked very little about personal relations between the sexes, at least not in mixed company and never very explicitly, but I suppose accurate description of what went on would have been as difficult then as at any time before or since.

There was once something of a scandal when some boys about 14 or 15 years old seized another boy and stuck the tube of a bicycle pump up his anus with the intention of inflating him. Of course they lacked the right kind of non-return valve, and the experiment failed. Surprisingly the victim was not a weakling but a strong, spirited lad whose brother pitched a fast curve ball for the Strathmore baseball team. He managed to escape, and he told his father what had happened. In those days there was no juvenile court in a place like Strathmore. There were not even police. The boy's father went to the attackers' fathers and demanded justice. The fathers had no doubts about the evil done. Afterwards a stocky, powerfully built butcher, who could throw a steer with his hands, said: "I gave my kid a thrashing he'll never forget." This I can well believe.

9

In the six years between the autumn of 1917 and the autumn of 1923 I had learned a new trade and established myself in an industry which showed some prospect of expansion, based upon the need for its products. There were, however, several elements in my situation which needed thinking about. In the first place my wife did not like Strathmore and her life on the C.P.R. Farm. Why should she? Strathmore and the Farm meant for her slavery and a denial of the normal aspirations of someone born and brought up in London, Ontario. Then there was the matter of our children: four of them by 1923. There was no doubt about the fact that children received a better education in city schools than in country schools, even allowing for the fact good teachers and good schools, and bad teachers and bad schools existed everywhere. If we thought beyond High School, then we could not remain in Strathmore, given my income and the cost of sending children away to a university. In fact, we never thought very concretely that far ahead.

As far as the C.P.R. Supply Farm was concerned, I liked what I was doing there and I was proud of what I had done. It seemed pretty obvious, however, that the Company was not going to invest any further resources in the Farm or the Irrigation system. An elementary need like a piped water supply was something I had to provide for myself in an inadequate way with materials scrounged from scraps. The poultry farm did not possess and could not obtain any form of transport for independent use, and the horse drawn light wagon called a democrat shared with other departments of the Farm was a time wasting and unreliable means of transporting fragile shipments of eggs. For $500.00 a Ford truck could have been provided, but it was not.

J. G. Rutherford had left the management of the Immigration Department of the C.P.R. for a career in politics. His successor George Hutton, a man with a heavy moustache, who always wore a luxuriously long and glossy beaver coat in winter, had no knowledge of what the poultry farm was like before I took over. He took what I was doing for granted and seemed to suppose that productivity and profits in running the plant were part of the natural order of events. In any case he was a hog and cattle man. Cattle were serious. Chickens were a half humorous or contemptible element in farming, fit for the attention of women. No one ever made a movie with a poultry farmer as the hero, whereas cattle, they were big and strong and it took men to handle them. Of course men could go bankrupt looking after cattle just as easily as they could grain farming or poultry farming, and, as the depression of the 1930's was to prove, the women and men who looked after chickens made more money than the he-men who held them in contempt. They survived and a lot of the he-men did not.

All things considered I was attracted by the possibility of becoming an inspector of R.O.P. flocks in the Livestock Division of the Canadian Department of Agriculture. If I could get a government job we could live in Calgary, and I would have a secure income: not large but secure. I can see now that I could also have gone into the poultry business on my own, either into hatching or into egg production. I knew enough about the production side to make good, and through my experience of selling day-old-chicks and breeding stock, I had a list of customers who bought from me and not from the C.P.R. even though they paid their money to the railway. But I had no capital. Worse, I had no confidence in myself as a business man, and I lacked a knowledge of finance and of people who could back me. I had already asked my wife's family and my own for help in difficulty, and I could not bring myself to ask again. On the whole the Government service seemed the best for me, if I could get a post.

Getting a post in the Dominion (that splendid word was used in those days) Civil Service was a matter of passing examinations set by the Civil Service Commission. Anybody could apply for a post and take the examination but the results suggested that college graduates did better than others. I had had very little schooling. I had never been to High School, let alone a university or agricultural college. However, I was self taught; I had a lot of practical experience and I understood the essentials of my trade. I decided to try the examinations. These involved written work and a demonstration of a practical knowledge of the Standard of Perfection, a description of the breeds of poultry; of practices like culling; of estimating egg laying capacity from an examination of hens; of the management of breeding processes; of candling eggs and so on. I was light on theory and on knowledge of subjects unconnected directly with poultry, but I was strong on the practical side.

There was one post going, and I stood second in the examination. The man who passed first, Clifford Barry, was a graduate of a well known agricultural college. Fortunately for me, Cliff Barry decided to take a job offered him in California. I was appointed. Cliff, however, did not stay in California, and returned to Canada where he took a job in the Dominion Department of Agriculture. Of all the men I ever worked with or worked under, I think Cliff Barry was the best, the most intelligent, the most capable and the most decent fellow I ever encountered. He was a splendid public servant, the kind of man who helps to make Canada a good country to live in.

When the C.P.R. heard I was leaving, the head office in Calgary turned nasty. I gave a month's notice according to normal practice and our original agreement. A few months previously the Alberta legislature had passed a law requiring employers to give employees two weeks terminal pay. Taking advantage of this law, the C.P.R. gave me my C.G. (or notice

131

with cash given) and two weeks pay and that was that. The bonus owing me was never paid. A few years after my departure the C.P.R.'s Poultry farm fell to pieces, and I always thought the C.P.R. got what they deserved. But a big organization can often act meanly without this having much effect except on its victims.

At the beginning of October, 1923, we moved back to Calgary, and established ourselves on 11th Avenue North East on the other side of the street from the house where we had been neighbours of Warren Hastings and his wife Phyllis. We were one door away from 6th Street N.E., which was then the furthest edge of the city. Beyond 6th Street lay a half section which was sown to wheat by a share cropping farmer. In 1927–28 this field was used by the aeroplanes which carried the first Canadian Air Mail. They landed on the stubble finding their direction into the wind by a wind sock in one corner of the field. The planes, which had Wright Whirlwind Radial engines, taxied up to some tiny sheds and in winter stuck their noses in them to keep warm, so that the frost would not cause their lubrication systems to seize up.

The community into which we moved on the North Hill was, like that in Strathmore, predominantly Anglo-Saxon of Canadian and American origins. Names not of Scottish, English or Irish derivation were few enough to be noticed. The only family of Jews bore the name of Hector, and they ran a machine shop where they repaired motor cars and well drilling equipment. For the most part the people on the North Hill were railway employees, school teachers, policemen, post office workers, barbers, shop keepers, salesmen, office workers and so on. Some achieved prominence. One man, James Watson, became Mayor of Calgary. He was a trade unionist and a pacifist. My eldest son was at that time a great reader of patriotic books about heroism such as *Deeds That Won the Empire*, and the life of Billy Bishop, V.C., Croix de Guerre and so on. One day Harry went for a Sunday walk with Mr. Watson, and was shocked and amazed to learn that military heroism and extravagant patriotism were not the finest and most admirable of qualities and that war, far from being the most noble of all activities, was the most degrading and horrible.

One of the youngsters frequently around our home in the mid-1920's, who became a prominent politician in Alberta, was Fred Peacock. The children of William Irvine, one of the leaders of the United Farmers of Alberta, attended Stanley Jones School when our children were there, and in 1927 Irvine's son and mine were the "commanding officers" of the Stanley Jones School Cadet Corps.

The most celebrated politician of the North Hill community was, however, William Aberhart, the founder of the Social Credit movement in Alberta, and the Premier of Alberta from 1935 to 1943. He was the Principal of Crescent Heights High School, which my son entered in September, 1927. He ran an excellent school, and parents from all over Calgary made special and mostly unsuccessful efforts to get their children in Crescent Heights on account of the school's record of examination successes. He was known by the students of Crescent Heights as Billy Balloon-Head, but he had their respect and was a terror to the rougher, tougher youngsters. Even in 1927 Aberhart was known to a larger public as a radio preacher and the head of the Canadian Bible Institute, a sort of do-it-yourself church based on fundamentalist doctrines somewhat similar to those of Jehovah's Witnesses. Aberhart's specialities were algebra, which he taught very competently, and prophecy in which field he was more often wrong than in mathematics.

By 1923 Calgary had revived a little, but not much from the catastrophe of 1913. Houses still stood empty, and rents were low. The building lots which I had once thought I owned were still building lots, and the board sidewalks which had given the sub-divisions the promise of inhabitation were rotting and weed grown excrescences on the prairie. A handsome bridge across the Bow River at Centre Street had, however, been built, and this seemed a sign that some people somewhere still had faith in Calgary.

There was a limited revival of optimism which set in about the time of our return to Calgary, and for a time it looked to me as if the excitement of 1905–1912 would explode once more. This revival was based on oil. Gas had been discovered in Turner Valley south of Calgary and at Bow Island near Lethbridge, and one of the advantages of living in Calgary was the abundance of cheap gas for domestic heating purposes. Where there was gas there must be oil, and where there is oil there is wealth. So the reasoning ran, and there was some truth in this. Unfortunately the deposits of oil were not easily reached with the drilling equipment then available, and the deposits when reached were not comparable with those in Texas and California as many hoped, and almost as many believed. When Royalite No. 4 blew in there was great excitement. The glow of burning gas in Turner Valley could be seen at night in Calgary, and this seemed to light men to paradise. Oil stocks were traded at 1 and 2 cents a share, and some stocks were quoted at figures as high as $25.00 a share. Along Eighth Avenue there were bucket shops peddling oil shares where before World War One there had been land offices luring in the suckers for a stripping.

All this did not affect me. I was a resident of Calgary; no longer a true believer in Calgary. In fact I was not much a resident. My new work obliged me to travel almost constantly between Fort William at the head of the lakes to Vancouver Island. I was never in Calgary for more than a week or two at a time except during holidays and once for an anxious month in 1924, when I was ordered home from Fort William and lived without salary while W. A. Brown, the head of the R.O.P. project, fought for its life against the economy minded, cheese paring politician, Mackenzie King.

The word inspector suggests bureaucratic snooping and the iron hand of government. An R.O.P. inspector was paid by the government and he was obliged to enforce the rules laid down by the Livestock Division of the Department of Agriculture, but he was never a bureaucrat or an authoritarian. Certainly I never was, and I never knew an R.O.P. inspector who had a reputation described by the words. An R.O.P. inspector was a worker in the poultry industry helping poultry breeders to help themselves. Everyone understood this. There was very little cheating by participants and the authority of government was very little used and seldom needed to be used. The routine of inspection was the means of getting to know the flock and its owner and to understand the strengths and weaknesses of both. What started as an inspection ended up as a consultation in which both the inspector and the inspectee learned from each other. I had had to learn poultry breeding by doing, and this experience enabled me to see problems from the producer's angle and to suggest ways of tackling problems which took account of the fact that the man or woman managing a flock was going through an experience of learning which I had had to go through myself. There were very few R.O.P. breeders whom I did not like and could not call friends, and I think that worked both ways. Even the big operators like George Solly on Vancouver Island who was a wealthy and successful man of long experience in the business and of high technical capacity, welcomed a visit from the R.O.P. inspector because such men and women were interested in their business and not above learning and teaching.

The routine of inspection was designed to test the accuracy of the records of performance kept by the participant in the scheme. Depending on the size of the flock entered in R.O.P. inspectors were present for twelve hours of a working day on at least eight to twelve days during a year. The rest of the time the R.O.P. poultry breeder kept his or her own records on the basis of which a certificate of a hen's capacity to lay eggs was issued by an agency of the Crown in Canada. Such certificates were worth money in terms of the sale of breeding stock.

The temptation to fake production figures was always there, and the main business of the inspector was to see that this did not happen. The existence of the inspection system was itself a safeguard against falsification. The inspector might appear at any time unannounced. When he arrived at 9 a.m. he took charge of the birds entered for certificates of performance for the rest of the day, and for as many days as the size of the entry required. He attended the trap nests, and made the records for the day. He examined the hens individually. Manual examination revealed whether or not a hen was laying eggs, although such an examination did not reveal exactly for how long this had been happening. But information obtained in this way threw some light on the reliability of the record set down for a particular hen. If a hen had a hard dried up pelvic area and the record showed recent egglaying, a question could properly be asked and an explanation required. Another check was the correspondence of the total production for a day with the total production of the previous day or selected days since the last inspection. Then there was the "expected to lay next day" test. Manual examination showed with a high degree of accuracy whether a hen would lay an egg within 12 to 24 hours. An inspector kept a record of the positive and negative expectations of a sample of hens, and then checked this against the reports of the breeder for the two days following his departure from the scene. It was possible, too, to make a general judgment of record keeping by looking at the health of the flock, the conditions under which the hens were kept and the state of the physical equipment such as the trap nests. Hens like people do not perform well if they are ill housed, ill fed and obliged to live disordered lives on account of the irresponsibility and incompetence of their masters, and there was usually a close correspondence between performance of the hens and the performance of their owners in the matter of care, order and cleanliness in essentials. If there was a serious discrepancy between one and the other an inspector was prompted to enquire further.

While there was probably a little marginal cheating here

and there, the main effect of the inspection system was to raise standards and hence productivity. The participants in the scheme had the same objectives as the government servants who organized it. The inspector was not someone to be out-witted and the breeders were not objects of regulation for the sake of regulation and for the exercise of authority by officials. The R.O.P. breeders were often animated by a real zest for competition, not for the making of money, but just for the satisfaction of being the possessor of hens that could lay more eggs than someone else's hens. When Mrs. J. H. McLardy of Miami, Manitoba, had her picture put on the cover of the annual catalogue of the R.O.P. Breeders' Association of Man-itoba with the first hen in Manitoba to lay more than 300 eggs in a year (this was in 1929) it was the equivalent of giving her a medal or an honorary degree, and she got as much satisfac-tion from this as she did from anything else that ever hap-pened to her.

I knew the R.O.P. system only as it existed west of the Great Lakes. In Ontario and Quebec commercial poultry pro-duction in the 1920's was much more developed than in west-ern Canada, and there the opportunities presented by R.O.P. were siezed upon more widely. In the west Manitoba and Brit-ish Columbia were the most interested areas—particulary Brit-ish Columbia where mixed farming—poultry, fruit, dairy cattle and so on—were the way to well being. On the prairies the dominance of wheat and limited nature of markets and the long distances one had to ship produce which had to be mar-keted shortly after production were obstacles to development. In Alberta, the provincial government agencies in the field of poultry promotion competed with those of the federal govern-ment. This reduced somewhat the appeal of R.O.P. in that pro-vince, but, of course, this did not adversely affect the develop-ment of the poultry industry there.

When the R.O.P. scheme started in the year 1919–1920 there were only three entries amounting to 203 hens in Man-itoba. This dropped to one entry and 25 hens the next year, but by 1928—29 there were 30 entries amounting to 2,450 birds. In British Columbia the figures both for entries and for growth were much more impressive. Professor Lloyd of the University of British Columbia was a strong supporter of the scheme, and he was well known to poultry men on account of his contribution to knowledge in the field of poultry husbandry. By 1925 there were more than 50 entries on Vancouver Island. In British Columbia, too, especially on Vancouver Island and in the Fraser Valley there was a much bigger investment of capital in the poultry industry than on the prairies. Some producers had very big flocks which exceeded even then what is nowadays regarded as the economically viable minimum of 10,000 birds.

Generally speaking, however, the poultry producers of western Canada were farmers, and more often farmer's wives, who were endeavouring to extend the range of their productive activities and to reduce their dependence on cereal farming as the sole source of their incomes. Of course, in some areas like the interior of British Columbia, large scale cereal production was never tried, and poultry was one of several other productive possibilities. In some other areas like, for example, the region between Lakes Manitoba and Winnipeg, cereal farming had been tried and had failed as an overall solution of the problem of earning a living. When the depression of 1929 brought the collapse of grain prices, poultry then began to look like a real and necessary means of adding to income everywhere except in the drought ravaged parts of eastern Alberta, southern Saskatchewan and the south western corner of Manitoba where there were no options of any kind.

Women played a substantial part in the development of the poultry industry in western Canada, and not just as skilful manual workers such as the women employed to candle eggs, pluck chickens and break eggs for canning purposes. Women organized and ran an important part of the poultry industry, and they occupied a leading position in the organization of the industry. It was to the initiative, perseverance, foresight, self discipline and powers of invention of women, most of them the wives of farmers, that the R.O.P. system was a success. A roll call of the women who were in large measure responsible for adding an important dimension to productivity in Western Canada would be a long one. I recall in particular Mrs. R. McNab and her daughter Grace and Mrs. E. J. Strahl of Minnedosa, Manitoba, Mrs. A McLardy of Miami, Manitoba, and Miss Harriet Purdy of Balcarres, Saskatchewan. Two of three directors of the R.O.P. Breeders Association of Manitoba in the 1930's were women: Miss Ellen Jickling of Dugald, Manitoba, and Mrs. W. G. Lacey of Rorketon. Mrs. J. Allen of Eriksdale, Manitoba, was one of the ablest breeders and organizers I encountered anywhere. God Bless them, every one.

As the industry grew men began to discover that their wives were making more money from the breeding of poultry than they were from the he-man activities of cattle raising and grain farming. They began to move into the industry and by the late 1930's occupied a dominant part in the business. This had, in my opinion, very little to do with technical ability or business capacity on the part of men. I think it was due very largely to male prejudice in the matter of finance. Banks do not take women as seriously as they do men; at least they did not in those days. Once the industry began to need finance for expansion women were at a disadvantage. This is illustrated in the field of hatching. There is no reason why women could not have done as well in hatching as they did in breeding, and one or two women did prove this to be the case. But women were of comparatively little importance in the hatching business, not for psychological reasons or for reasons of ability, but because hatching requires more capital equipment to start any scale of operation than breeding does. Hence finance is more important to hatchers than to breeders, at least in the early stages, and women could never get a square shake from the money lenders. As breeders, however, they never had to go near a bank, and could parley a few hundred dollars into a few thousand by hard work, intelligence and patience.

There was one thing I noticed about women in the poultry industry. While there were notable exceptions it seemed generally to be the case that good female poultry keepers were seldom good housekeepers. They were outdoor types. When inspecting a female breeder's flock one could be pretty sure that one would not get a good meal in a comfortable farm kitchen. I was once talking to another inspector about a woman who had a good flock of birds, and we got around to the terrible quality of her cooking. I said on her behalf that she did bake bread. "Hell," said my fellow official, "she doesn't bake; she vulcanizes."

My activities as an inspector were directed from Ottawa. The men in charge of Poultry Division in the capital were W.A. Brown, the Chief of the Division, and R. W. Zavitz, the supervisor of Record of Performance. The set-up was very simple, and little manpower was wasted on administration. "Rusty" Zavitz sent the inspectors their itineraries, which were instructions about the poultry farms of entrants which were to be visited for a period of about three to four weeks, with dates of the visits specified. Every year in the autumn an inspector visited the plants of entrants in order to pass and band the flock for entry. This involved certifying hens for entry which were judged to be pure bred and meeting the requirements of the *Standard of Perfection*, a standard established by poultry fanciers, but not necessarily good layers and vice versa. After all hens are like women. A model in *Harpers Bazaar* probably represents some sort of perfection but it does not follow that she will produce the maximum number of children, or the maximum of anything. She just has a perfect appearance. So with a hen in the *Standard of Perfection* of the poultry fanciers.

My first and only run-in with W. A. Brown, for which he appeared never to forgive me, was connected with applying the rules about the *Standard of Perfection*. I did not believe in the *Standard of Perfection* as the bible of the poultry business, nor

140

did he. But the rules were the rules, something like the more arbitrary bits of the Book of Deuteronomy. I was instructed to pass for entry and band a flock of birds owned by a distinguished and socially important medical doctor in Calgary. This man or his wife, I never discovered which, had purchased the stock from a poultry breeder in Ontario. I looked at them carefully and I was sorry to have to tell the distinguished doctor that his flock did not measure up to the *Standard of Perfection:* ragged feathers, too off colour in the plumage, legs not the right colour and so on. The doctor and his wife complained to W. A. Brown in Ottawa. He sent me a telegram and I sent him telegrams. In as many ways as possible he told me to band the doctor's flock, and to hell with the rules, but he never came right out and said this. I took the line that the rules were the rules, and if I bent them for the doc I would soon have to bend them for others. Actually the doctor did not care very much about the matter and was prepared to agree with me, but his wife could not stomach the idea of the government of Canada denying her anything she wanted. The upshot was that the rules were enforced, but at the cost of the good will of W. A. Brown for me. As I learned later Brown was under a lot of political pressure from his enemies in Ottawa, and he needed friends. This doctor in Calgary was more influential than most R.O.P. entrants on the prairies and Brown wanted his support. He was put into a terrible dilemma by stiff-necked adherence to a rule I did not myself believe was very important. His whole system depended on rules, but his survival depended on friends. I was too inexperienced to understand this, and he never was cordial towards me for the rest of my time under his direction.

In all my time I never visited Ottawa. Occasionally R.O.P. inspectors west of the Lakes were called together for a discussion. My first visit to the west coast was for this purpose. By and large an inspector was on his own. If satisfaction is to be measured by non-interference and the absence of adverse comment on what I did, I seem to have met all the requirements of my job.

My pay was little better than I had finally achieved with the C.P.R., but I did get all my expenses paid while travelling away from home. These covered train fares, liveries, i.e. travel to and from the nearest station by car, horse and buggy or horse and sleigh, meals and hotel accommodation. I was able to live on my expenses and to turn over my salary cheque completely to my wife for the maintenance of my family. I clothed myself by much walking and so saving livery fares. All expenses had to be accounted for, and it was a tedious boring job each month to work out a detailed expense account. What took me a day a month to do must have taken a man in Ottawa as long to check. I always thought that the estimated average cost per day could have been worked out, and the number of days on the road multiplied by the average cost per day in order to pay inspectors a lump sum which they could spend as they wanted — to dig into their own resources to stay at the Royal Alexandra or augment their income by staying in the Hotel Fleabag. But that was not Ottawa's way. Somebody needed a job, and what better way to provide one than by appointing a man to count receipts and scrutinize expenses. In spite of this I never spent more than the rules allowed, and I never claimed for less, and no expense account ever back fired on me. And I did a lot of very enjoyable walking in western Canada saving on liveries.

Doing the kind of work I did, I came to know the small towns of the prairies very well. One of the hardships of the job was the hotels and eating places. Prohibition had a serious effect on the hotel business throughout the west from its imposition by the several provincial governments during World War I until its abolition during the depression of the 1930's. Prohibition did not stop the drinking of liquor, beer and wines, but it did divert the revenues of the business out of the pockets of hotel keepers into the pockets of bootleggers who handled the stuff illegally and the druggists who were allowed to sell whisky, brandy, gin, etc. on prescription for medical purposes. There was a very great increase in illnesses which could only be cured by a slug of liquor, but the profits from this form of cure did not go to the hotel keepers. The result of this impairment of the income of hotel keepers by prohibition was a lack of investment of capital and a decline in standards of accommodation so that in some towns one was lucky to find a room over the Chinese restaurant.

Indeed I once found myself in bed with a Chinese gentleman as a consequence of there being no hotel in Winnifred, Alberta. It happened like this in the autumn of 1925. Winnifred was more or less a ghost town on the railway line between Medicine Hat and Lethbridge. This was my first visit. The train west used to arrive there about 2 a.m. and an hour later the eastbound train, and I could find no hotel. I went back to the station, lay down on a seat in the waiting room with my coat wrapped around me and went to sleep. I was no sooner asleep than a man shone a torch in my face and asked me what I was doing in the station at that hour. He had come to get the mail off the eastbound train. I told him and he said: "See that light over there? That's my place. You can sleep there, and any time you're in this neck of the woods, why just come in and bed down." We went back to his place. I went to bed, and slept until 8 o'clock or so.

Three months later I again got off the train at Winnifred, Alberta, saw the light of the house and made for it. I went in. There was no one about, but there was a good fire in the stove and the place was warm. I undressed; put on my pyjamas and went to bed; pretty soon a man came and said to me, "Hey, you're in my bed. There's one upstairs." And so I went upstairs and went to bed on a couch. Again, a man disturbed me and said, "You're in my bed." I got out and groped about and found a double bed, got in and went to sleep. I slept pretty soundly, and wakened about 8 o'clock, turned over and found another man in bed with me. I climbed out, and in so doing, wakened my bedfellow. He threw back the covers. He was

Chinese. "Who are you?" he asked. A good question. It turned out that the man who had invited me to put up in his place had sold out to a new man who boarded people in his house. Every one had been at a party when I arrived, and had returned one by one, the last man being the Chinese, who ran the only restaurant in Winnifred. He is the one I had slept with.

Probably the worst hotel on the prairies was at Ochre River, Manitoba. It was owned by an old Englishman. He had a mad daughter whom he kept locked up in a room at the end of a corridor. When it rained, the proprietor used to put tin cans along the corridor of the top floor to catch the drips of rain coming through the roof. All night long one could hear the splash, splash of water dropping into tin cans. This night it was raining and I was working by the light of an oil lamp in my room, writing a report. Above the drips of water I could hear the squeaking of the door. I turned around as it slowly opened. The mad daughter entered. She was tall and thin with staring eyes and unkempt hair, and she wore a long flannel night gown. "I want my father," she said slowly with great deliberation. "I want my father." I felt as though I had had an overdose of Lady Macbeth.

If the hotel at Ochre River was the worst in the west, the hotel at Davidson, Saskatchewan, was probably the coldest. This was not due to prohibition, but to the system of heating. The lobby of the hotel was in the centre of the building and the rooms were located on corridors which ran left and right from the lobby. The architect, if there was one, had the idea that the heat there would diffuse through transoms to the bedrooms. This did not happen, with the result that the bedrooms were hideously cold. I used to sleep in my overcoat and overshoes in this hotel.

I heard this story from one of the characters in it. The train to Saskatoon stopped at Davidson in the middle of the night, and passengers awaiting the train often stopped in the lobby of the hotel to keep warm. One night a travelling sales-

144

man who could not endure the cold in his bedroom, moved down to the lobby and went to sleep on a sofa, warm if not comfortable. This night the thermometer was about -30 F. Ten minutes or so before the train arrived, a man in a long buffalo coat and fur hat came into the lobby. He had driven 10 miles or so and his cap, moustache and the collar of his coat were covered with ice and frost particles as a result of the water vapour of his breath freezing. He stamped his feet, to shake off the snow from his boots, and warm his feet. This wakened the sleeping salesman. He looked at the newcomer. "God Almighty," he exclaimed. "What room did they put you in?"

Another story told of cold hotel rooms concerned a travelling salesman who, before going to bed, put his false teeth in the large jug of water used for washing and shaving. He overslept, and upon getting up discovered that his train was due within minutes. He threw on his clothes, stuffed his things in his suitcase and turned to get his false teeth. They were frozen solid in a block of ice in the water jug. The whistle of the train sounded in the distance. What to do? The salesman threw on his overcoat, grabbed his suitcase in one hand and the water jug in the other, and rushed for the station. He was last seen boarding the local hugging a jug containing false teeth embedded in three pounds of ice while the trainman handed up his suitcase.

While bad hotels were one of the hazards of my work, there were, too, some good ones. The Tremont in Minnedosa, Manitoba, was the cleanest and warmest hotel in western Canada, and if I had been asked whether I preferred the Tremont in Minnedosa to the Palliser in Calgary, there would have been no doubt in my mind about the answer: The Tremont. Its owner-manager was Jim Rae. He was one of Manitoba's great eccentrics. His eccentricities were not just oddities of behaviour but touched upon serious public issues, which public relations minded business men are supposed to avoid. For example, his son Cliff was called up for compulsory military service during World War I. As a protest Jim Rae closed his hotel down for the duration of the war, boarded it up and moved his wife and family into a cottage, while he went off to play the stock market. When he reopened after the Armistice he discovered he had left more than $10,000 in the hotel safe. He had simply forgotten he had this money.

Minnedosa is located in a deep valley on the main line of the C.P.R. from Winnipeg to Edmonton. In those days before the town of Thompson was built in northern Manitoba, Minnedosa enjoyed a reputation along with White River, Ontario, of being the coldest town in Canada. When it was -40 F, what a relief to return from a farm to a room in The Tremont, where the steam radiators were fairly bursting to greet you, and where you could sit down in Jim Rae's immaculately clean dining room to a good solid, well cooked meal! Jim was proud of his hotel, and he did not take kindly to people who supposed that it was anything but the best. One day a young, inexperienced but self confident salesman arrived at The Tremont for the first time. He came up to the desk, put down his bags and banged the bell for attention. Jim Rae looked up from his accounts.

"I want the best room in the house," the young man said. Jim said nothing. He got up, came around the desk, picked up the young man's bags, carried them to the front door, and pitched them into the street.

"All my rooms are the best," he roared.

In spite of the strong family feeling which caused Jim Rae to close his hotel in protest against the taking of his son, he never spoke to his wife, nor she to him; at least I never saw them exchange a word, and no one of my acquaintance ever did. His family ate at a table next to the door between the dining room and kitchen. Mrs. Rae and one or other of the children would come and take their meal. Jim would appear later. Sometimes he dined with his children, but never with his wife.

In addition to the warmth and cleanliness of The Tremont and the eccentricities of its proprietor, I remember, too, that on one of its walls inscribed in a way which made removal difficult was the only example of lavatorial verse which seems to me to merit recording. It went like this:

"In the Houses which govern our land,
When a motion is made the members stand.
In this little house we are far better treated;
When a motion is made the member is seated."

A man in Minnedosa worth knowing was Art Gray. He ran one of several livery stables in the town. In those days, and indeed until after World War II, there were only two practical means of travel in Manitoba in winter: by train for distances over 15—20 miles and by horse and sleigh for distances less than this. I used to have to spend a week or more in the Minnedosa area and was obliged to visit farms as much as ten or twelve miles distant from the town. In weather always well below zero and often as low as -30 F and sometimes -40 F, travelling was no fun unless one did business with Art Gray. He perfected a horse drawn vehicle which was known locally as a cab. This was a sleigh or cutter completely roofed in with heavy canvas having only small celluloid windows, and a small slit through which the reins passed. Inside there was a charcoal footwarmer and a farm lantern for warmth. Provided one let the horses go at their own pace a journey by cab was comfortable and safe, and immensely better than journeying in an open cutter depending for warmth on a fur coat, mitts, hat, scarves and overshoes.

In summer Art Gray was equally dependable. He could get you anywhere with a model T. This was a matter of knowing the roads which were not all built or maintained up to a standard fit for travel even in dry weather. The sloughs around Minnedosa made it good country for hunting ducks, but a difficult one for the motorist so that even a journey of 30-40 miles to Brandon was a hazardous and uncertain undertaking.

Although most of my work took me from prairie town to prairie town from the foothills of the Rockies to Lake Superior and from north of Edmonton to towns near the Canadian boundary, I spent some time in British Columbia, and on one occasion was away from home for nearly six months on Vancouver Island, up and down the Fraser Valley, in the Okanagan and so on. B.C. was a new experience for me; not only the scenery but the people and their way of doing things. Although the people spoke English and were in the main of Anglo-Saxon descent in those days, British Columbia was in many ways a very different society from that on the prairies and in Ontario. I could never quite figure this out. In some ways the interior of British Columbia was poorer than the prairies, and many people lived a sort of hill billy existence. When I used to remark on the beauty of the scenery, more than one replied, "Yeah, but you can't live on the scenery." There were a number of ghost towns nearly dead like Slocan City. These had flourished on the strength of mines which had run out. The people left behind scratched a living with a few fruit trees, a vegetable patch and a few hens and maybe a cow or a pig. They demonstrated what the ideal of forty acres of mixed farming, which the C.P.R. had tried to sell in Alberta, was really like. They could sell little of the products of their labour, and what they did sell was eaten up in freight charges. The railway did all right, but the people did not.

I once had an illustration of this. I was inspecting a small poultry plant near Creston B.C. The owner had an orchard. He had picked and packed his apple crop, but the tops of the trees were loaded with marvellous fruit. I asked him why this was. He explained that picking at the top of the tree required ladders, and the job was not worth the effort and expense. I asked if I could have some of the apples to send home. "Go ahead," the man said, "Take as many as you like. Here's a crate to put them in.'

I climbed the apple tree with a basket and soon filled the crate, took it to the station, and despatched it to my wife in Calgary express by baggage car. When my wife wrote me next, she told me that the apples were the best she had had for years, but that the express charges made the apples more expensive than the ones she was buying in the Calgary market.

That was the kind of thing the farmers in the interior of B.C. were up against, at a time when the railway brotherhoods saw to it that their members made $200 and $300 a month, and the C.P.R. shares were selling at more than $100 a piece on the Montreal and London Stock exchanges.

If the interior of B.C. was poor in those days, this was not the case in the Fraser Valley and on Vancouver Island. Here was a different world. Not a few of the poultry farmers there were retired officers of the British and Canadian armed forces. None of them were playing at poultry farming, but they had capital and they had markets close at hand: Vancouver and Victoria and Seattle and Portland in the United States. The railways got comparatively little of what they produced.

In the homes of the poultrymen of Vancouver Island and the Fraser Valley, I encountered for the first time a new way of life. Back in Ontario and on the prairies most people had parlours or sitting rooms in their homes, but these were seldom used. The furniture was polished and dusted, but it was never used except maybe at Christmas or at the time of a baptism or a funeral. These people on Vancouver Island, Salt Spring Island and in the Fraser Valley really lived in their living rooms. What a nice life it was: comfortable, well used easy chairs, tea about 4:30 p.m., a smoke and a chat; and maybe a little music on the victrola or someone playing the piano. There were real flower gardens and lawns and sometimes tennis courts. Some of the Churchill family had a place on Salt Spring Island, and they had a tennis court made of planks built on to the side of the low, rocky cliffs which looked out to the straits between the island and the mainland.

And there I met people of a kind hitherto unknown to me. One time I was instructed to inspect the flock of an R.O.P. breeder at Cobble Hill near Shawnigan Lake. I arrived at the normal time, and all day this man and I worked together. Like any working farmer he was dressed in a work shirt and denim overalls stained with chicken feed, dung and machine oil. About 4, we had a cup of tea standing in his kitchen, which he made himself, being a bachelor. About 5:30 he invited me into his sitting room, asked me to stay to dinner, gave me a drink and indicated a pile of magazines to read if I so wished. He excused himself very politely. The sitting room was decorated with campaign flags from the Ashanti wars, the Boer War and other wars, and photographs of soldiers and soldiering. About an hour or more later my host appeared. He wore a starched white shirt, a black bow tie, and a short red coat with medal ribbons, which I learned was a mess jacket. He then ushered me into his dining room, and we proceeded to eat a five course meal, beautifully served, which he had prepared himself.

It turned out that this man was the colonel-in-chief of the Irish Guards, retired. He had fought in many wars, but what most he talked about was the action at Gallipoli, and the massacre on the beaches. For the first time I heard a man speak well of his enemies, for he praised the skill and courage of the Turks, whom he considered among the finest and bravest soldiers in his experience. This was news to me, because whenever I thought of Turks, which was seldom, I assumed them to be some sort of hideous barbarians who, when not flogging slaves, were enjoying the pleasures of the harem.

Another extraordinary military man I encountered was a Canadian. He was not a poultry breeder, but his daughter was. It transpired that the daughter was at the time of my visit to inspect her flock, vacationing in Hawaii. When I arrived I entered through some large ornamental iron gates, and came upon a large white haired man in the driveway.

"You're Mr. Gwynne?" I enquired.

The man drew himself up and roared at me. "General Gwynne! General Gwynne!"

He turned out to be a very decent sort. He, too, invited me to dinner. He kept a bottle of whisky on the table, which he drank neat from a fair sized wine glass and encouraged his guest to do the same. We became very good friends by about 10 p.m. and I learned a lot about Sir Sam Hughes, Sir Arthur Currie and the politics of Ottawa during the first World War all of which I regret I have now forgotten.

It was in the home of another military man that I had one of the more embarrassing experiences of my life and where I first saw a respectable woman smoke a cigarette. The military man was a retired colonel of the British Army. He was married to a lady rather younger than himself. After a day's work with the retired colonel he and his wife invited me to dinner. We had a very pleasant meal elegantly served. It was the custom on the prairies for a guest to offer around cigarettes after the conclusion of a meal. I took out my cigarettes and offered one to my host. He took one and I took one. Then his wife turned to her husband and said very politely, "Could you let me have a fag, please?" I can think of few occasions when I felt so ashamed of myself, and so completely and painfully snubbed.

British Columbia is a place of great natural beauty. It is also a place where human indifference to nature was even 50 years ago much in evidence. At Metchosin, on Vancouver Island, I came upon a great valley, which some years previously had been filled with magnificent trees hundreds of feet high. When I saw the valley it was a vast graveyard of black charred tree stumps from six to eight feet tall. One's heart broke at the general desolation; and one wondered at the waste of hundreds of thousands of board feet of timber contained in the stumps. I learned that the trees were cut so far above the ground because the hand operated saw of those days could not cut through the densely resinous wood at the base of the tree trunks, and the effective cuts had to be made well above ground level, the sawyers standing on spikes driven into the trees.

Mill Bay, where one took a launch to Pender Island, was in the 1920's a most beautiful place. When my wife and I visited Mill Bay 40 years later it had been ruined by the construction of a great cement plant nearby. Pender Island itself was a kind of paradise. There the people grew the finest pears one could ever eat: a variety not seen very often, which were ugly looking fruit and not very pear shaped, but of an unbelievable juiciness, sweetness and flavour.

Chemainus was another station in paradise. Here lived the man who had established the branch of the T. Eaton Company in Winnipeg in 1905 and had managed it for many years. He had located his splendid house on a bench of land above the sea, and down below his yacht was moored at a small jetty. Behind was an immense forest. In 1952 this was all cut down leaving a scene of desolation. A special delight in Chemainus, apart from the landscape and seascape was strawberries and cream, served by an English innkeeper, who had his own strawberry patch and kept a small herd of Jersey cows.

The coast of Vancouver Island facing the mainland had many beautiful beaches, but most of these were piled high with endless palisades of logs which had escaped from the loggers. These were an immense resource which could have been used locally, but the logging companies prosecuted beachcombers who touched what they claimed was their property.

At Sproat Lake near Alberni a logging company was laying out a tree cutting operation that was intended to last for 25 years. Here there was an incredible, unbelievable forest of immense trees which rose straight up densely packed together. Their trunks were bare of branches for ninety feet. The system for taking logs out, which would have been impossible at ground level on account of the density of the stumps, was to run cables fastened to the tops of the trees, and along these to convey the logs chained to pulleys. At Courtenay, while I was on Vancouver Island, there was a terrible forest fire caused by this method of taking out logs. A cable broke under great stress, and being overheated by friction set fire to a dry cedar around which it wrapped itself when it snapped.

On the coast at Cowichan Bay it was possible to sit on the dock at evening and hear the salmon flopping in the water. Twenty-five pounders were commonly taken by fishermen. One afternoon while I was stopping in Cowichan a traveller went out in a boat and hooked a salmon weighing 40 pounds. Everyone thought this trophy was bound to be mounted, but the man gave his catch to the hotel and told the manager to give his guests a good feed. This the manager did, and the result with parsley sauce was excellent.

In the 1920's there was a very popular painter of landscapes named Maxfield Parrish. Many people claimed he overdid it in the lush way he laid on his colours. Certainly to anyone living on the prairies Maxfield Parrish seemed either a liar in paint or a dream artist. But in the Okanagan Valley looking down on the lake there Maxfield Parrish seemed true to life. There was a wonderful beach at Penticton where a few people had summer houses or boarding houses and a large hotel for tourists who came in by railway or by boat. It was not possible to move through this part of British Columbia entirely by rail. One was obliged to take a train to Kuskanook if travelling from the east, and there take a boat to Nelson, where one caught the Kettle Valley Railway to Vancouver.

Passengers on the Kettle Valley Railway were obliged to sign a release from liability in the event of accidents. That these had happened was evident enough from the sight of skeletons of trains in the valleys far below the trestles on which the trains crossed from mountain to mountain. Every so far on these trestles were barrels of water for use in case of fire. While on the trestles the engineers kept the speed of the trains down, but once the engine reached *terra firma* the engineers opened the throttle. The coaches still on the trestles swayed as if whip lashed from a distance, and the water in the barrels slopped over the sides with the movement. Anyone frightened of air travel would get a sense of perspective, had they the opportunity to travel on the Kettle Valley Railway as it was a half century ago.

Down in the valleys were farms. But it was often a matter of farming with a crowbar, so rocky was the land. One could fall out of the farms which were situated higher up to take advantage of the pockets of soil on the sides of the mountains. At Appledale B.C. I encountered the poorest farmer I ever met, a religious Scot named Andrew Cant. How he ever financed a flock of R.O.P. chickens and managed the entrance fee of $15.00 I shall never know. And yet he survived by hard work and ingenuity. He offered me a meal which reminded me of the grub I ate in Calgary when I was fighting for survival. The only difference was that Andrew Cant did not have five cents for canned beans. When the meal was over I said I wanted to pay him at the top rate allowed for an R.O.P. inspector's dinner by the Treasury in Ottawa. He accepted gratefully. That was the first Federal subsidy this man had had in his life.

One of the more interesting entrants in R.O.P. was Major H. G. L. Strange, who was something of a minor celebrity in Western Canada in the 1920's and 30's. When I first met him he operated a large farm at Fenn, Alberta. It was here that he grew the wheat which won him the title of World Wheat Champion. He was an Englishman, born in Stepney in London. The rank of Major he had attained in a unit which developed gas warfare. After the war he went to Hawaii where he married a young Kanaka girl, who bore him two large, dark sons, Bob and Harry. Bob died young but Harry eventually ended up as a reporter on the *Chicago Tribune*. When Major Strange's wife died, he moved to California where he married Kathleen Redman-Strange who developed a reputation of her own as a journalist, and as the author of a well known book about life on the prairies—*With the West in Her Eyes.* In the course of his knocking around the world Major Strange persuaded a group of English investors to buy land in Canada and to appoint him to select the purchases by scientific and statistical methods. The farm at Fenn, Alberta, was one of his selections, and this he was appointed to manage. How successful an enterprise the farm was I do not know. I would guess it was not, judging by the large number of ineffective workers he employed. These were all "green Englishmen" who did not learn much about farming but acclimatized themselves to Canada and its ways at Fenn, before moving on to other careers, mainly in the cities.

154

He did, however, employ these men to good effect in winning the world wheat championship, because he enlisted them to sit around a great table covered with wheat, where under his direction his winning wheat sample was selected and polished grain by grain.

After winning the wheat title Major Strange moved from farming to editing a trade paper for a grain company, and became what is known as a public relations man. Always a great talker and story teller he created a kind of myth about himself which people did not wholly believe. His attempt to imitate his wife's success as an author was a failure. An aspect of his unusual personality was the habit of disappearing from western Canada from time to time to travel by himself in Florida and the islands of the Caribbean.

One man I encountered on Major Strange's place at Fenn, was R. F. Fisher, who became a lifelong friend. I never called him anything but Fisher from the time I first met him in 1925 until he died in retirement in British Columbia in the 1950's. He had been an Egyptian civil servant in the days of British control in Egypt, and had served in Allenby's army in Palestine. He came to Canada after being defrauded of all his resources by a friend in England. For thirty years he worked as a poultryman on various farms from Alberta to the Great Lakes, and he lived a life of very great simplicity. He was one of those men, like myself, who discovered in birds and animals creatures which he understood better than human beings, and I think he found a happiness with them that he never knew in his life as an Egyptian Civil Servant. Fisher was always my idea of a gentleman.

10

I worked as an R.O.P. inspector from October, 1923, until November, 1928. During that time I visited or stopped off in Winnipeg whenever my itinerary took me into Manitoba and the far western end of Ontario. There I became acquainted with A. C. McCulloch, like me an official of the Poultry Division of the Canadian Department of Agriculture. Mac (I knew him for twenty years before I discovered that his Christian names were Arthur Clifford) held the office of Poultry Promoter, i.e. his job was what it said: to promote the development of the poultry industry in Manitoba in any way he could. He came from Uxbridge, Ontario, where his family had farmed for some generations. He himself attended the Ontario Agricultural College at Guelph, where he specialized in the study of poultry. Mac had energy, imagination, organizing ability and a capacity for hard work. He was a hard task master, but he never asked any man to do anything he would not and could not do himself. He was a man after my own heart. We were colleagues for twenty-seven years and, what is more difficult in the civil service, friends until his death in 1963. Mac's only mistake was to attempt to operate a poultry farm of his own at Portage la Prairie either in his spare time or with hired help; and this cost him a lot both in money and reputation.

By 1928 Mac had achieved so much success in his job and developed so many activities that he asked me whether I would be willing to join him in his work, if he could sell the idea of a second man in Manitoba to the higher-ups in Ottawa.

156

At this time I was ready for a change. Being based in Winnipeg and working in a smaller territory like Manitoba, I could be at home with my family more than was possible when I was travelling weeks at a time along the railways of western Canada. In Manitoba I would be able to travel about by car on a mileage allowance from the Government, and this had its attractions. The work would have more variety and I would be able to use more directly my knowledge of aspects of the industry such as hatching which was only incidental to my R.O.P. work. And there were family considerations. We now had five children and the eldest was within sight of finishing High School. In Winnipeg there was a university and in Calgary there was not. When I added everything up, I figured that the answer to McCullouch's offer was "Yes".

Mac succeeded in convincing the officials of the Department of Agriculture in Ottawa and they in turn convinced the Treasury Board that poultry promotion in Manitoba needed another man. It was agreed that I would work with Mac, but would be available for R.O.P. inspection work in Manitoba and eastern Saskatchewan and the Lakehead, if there was any need for assistance. It was further agreed that the government would pay the cost of moving my family and household goods to Winnipeg.

In the summer of 1929, during the school holidays we moved from Calgary to Winnipeg. I had been off and on in the town, usually either passing through or for a few days, since 1905. Between 1905 and World War I Winnipeg grew at great speed, and most of the main buildings and the general lay out of the city as it existed until the 1960's came into being during those years. From the end of the war in 1918 for forty years Winnipeg did not change much in physical appearance. There was, of course, some building in the suburbs, and here and there a few big buildings like the Hudson's Bay Company's store on Portage Avenue and the Winnipeg Auditorium were built, but in general Winnipeg stood still, at least to look at. Winnipeg had a reputation, which it still has to some extent, as a place which was stagnating. This stagnation was attributed to the building of the Panama Canal, which affected the movement of goods from east to west and west to east. It was attributed, too, to the General Strike of 1919, which was supposed to have frightened off investors of capital. There may be something in these ideas, but my view was then and still is that Winnipeg at that time was just like Calgary. It was overbuilt as a result of the kind of optimism about western Canada and the kind of greed for quick wealth which had caused me to fall flat on my little face in 1913–1915, and which had caused a lot of big men, too, to fall flat on their fat behinds at the same time. Winnipeg and Manitoba had had its self confidence destroyed just the same as I had my own destroyed. Mean, defeated and scared: that was the character of the Bracken Government in Manitoba and it was the character of the people like the Siftons who ran Winnipeg. Winnipeg and Manitoba eventually pulled out of their slough of despond, but this owed very little to the narrow minded, frightened penny pinchers who were in charge. The revival of Winnipeg and Manitoba was brought about by the little people: the outsiders, the Jews, the Ukrainians, the Mennonites, the Hutterites, the women on the farms and the poor farmers generally who worked hard, thought of new things to do and new things to study and had the guts to get somewhere. That's how I see it after living more than forty years in Manitoba.

I bought a house on Inkster Boulevard in the North End. The man after whom the street was named was then still alive, known by everyone as Sheriff Inkster. He had been for many years the High Sheriff of Manitoba He was born a British subject in the territory of the Hudson's Bay Company. During his lifetime he had witnessed the passing of the buffalo herds, the transfer of the Company's jurisdiction to the government of Canada, two Riel Rebellions, the establishment of the Province of Manitoba, the arrival of the railway, and the coming of automobiles, aeroplanes and the radio. He worshipped most Sundays in St. John's Catherdral being driven there by his daughter in a Willys Knight. He, Bob Jacob, Tom Morton, who were lawyers, and Bob Hamelyn and John Jack, whose daughter married our eldest son, always played poker every Friday night: rotating among each others houses. He lived in an old frame house with a large drawing room on North Main Street, and there was a monument outside his garden recalling the Battle of Seven Oaks which took place on the grounds of his residence. He died following an accident while duck hunting at the age of 91. He was part Indian and proud of it.

I am afraid my wife never liked me purchasing a house in the North End. But it wasn't a bad place to live. The schools were good: Luxton School, Machray School and St. John's Technical High School. St. John's Tech enjoyed no social prestige, but it was the best school in Winnipeg on account of good teachers and good students. The Principal was G. J. Reeve, an Englishman who had been at Oxford University. He was an easy going, tolerant man who ran a happy school and he took the view that making money was not the main thing in life. A high percentage of the boys and girls in St. John's Tech were Jews or Ukrainians. On Yom Kippur the student population in the school was so reduced that it was almost a holiday for the goys. Many graduates of the school came to occupy high positions in Canadian society: Sam Freedman became a judge and the Chancellor of the University of Manitoba. His brother Max was for many years the Washington correspondent of the *Manchester Guardian.* Louis Slotin was a nuclear scientist at Oak Ridge, and the first man, not Japanese, to die of radiation sickness from an accident during his research work. "Tubber" Kobrinsky became a well known physician after being a famous football player. Bohdan Hubicki was a star violinist, and went on to play in a symphony orchestra in London where he was killed in a German air raid. Eugene Nemish became an internationally known concert violinist. In the North End there was a music teacher of world class, John Melnyk.

The Jewish children nearly all came from homes where learning was respected. Many of them went to the Hebrew

School as well as to St. John's Tech and were able to read Hebrew as well as English. Most Jewish boys and girls were anxious to excel, and this created a competitive atmosphere good for the advancement of learning. Yes, St. John's Tech was not a bad place for kids to go to school, and I am glad that all my children went to Tech.

There was still in the North End, forty to fifty years ago some survivals of the generation which had helped to found Manitoba, clustered around St. John's Catherdral. S. P. Matheson, a man with an enormous beard was Archbishop of Rupertsland, and he lived in a big house on Scotia Street which ran along the banks of the Red River. St. John's College and St. John's College School were then located on North Main Street where there is now a great Auto Mart. One of the teachers at St. John's College and a Canon of the Cathedral was a young Englishman named H. G. G. Herklots. He had been president of the Union, a debating society at Cambridge University, and he wrote books not only on theological subjects but humorous essays, some of which were published in a collection entitled *Paper Aeroplanes,* and an account of his new life in Winnipeg entitled *The First Winter.* His wife, Helen, was an equally interesting and valuable member of the community. She was a medical doctor whose mother had been a fellow student of Dr. Marie Stopes, the pioneer of the birth control movement. Her father was a famous Roumanian geologist who had been one of the tutors of King Carol. She used to tell the story of how she and her husband were hitch hiking in the Balkans, and found themselves without money. This problem was solved by knocking on the gates of King Carol's palace in Bucharest, and getting from the King a hand-out sufficient to get them back to England.

St. John's College like the Church of England was hard hit by the Machray Scandal in the 1930's. It was discovered in 1932 that John A Machray, K.C., a nephew of the first Archbishop of Rupertsland and the honorary bursar both of the Church and the University of Manitoba, had systematically looted the Church and the University of its trust funds: $900,000 from the University and $800,000 from the Church and its College.

The influences brought to bear on young people varied a good deal. An old Anglo-Irish clergyman used to prepare boys of 16 or 17 for confirmation. On a subject superabundantly discussed nowadays he limited himself to saying: "At a certain stage in life boys have certain kinds of thoughts. When they do, they should go for a long walk." On the other hand, G. J. Reeve, who ran the Boys Bible Class made it into a forum for all sorts of discussion. He had the young students of the Bible read the *Intelligent Woman's Guide to Socialism* by George Bernard Shaw, and when the Bank of Canada was being set up by Parliament he arranged a lecture on banking. Once he invited one of the prominent leaders of the Jewish Community, Rabbi Solomon Frank, to speak to the boys on the evidence for the existence of God. I had never had the time nor the inclination to think this kind of discussion was necessary, and so I asked my son was was said. He told me that Rabbi Frank, who was a big dark, handsome man without a beard, simply took out his pocket watch, unlinked it from his gold watch chain and placed it on the table in front of him. He then said something like this: "Observe this watch ticking regularly and without stop. It serves a purpose. No one doubts but that it had a maker. I can even tell you his name. Look around you at the universe infinitely more complex and more wonderful than this watch. Can you suppose that it has no Maker? You cannot. I can tell you his name." Then he sat down and invited questions.

Starting to a new school inevitably generated tensions in our children. In order to relieve this, my wife and I took them to the Metropolitan Theatre on Donald Street opposite the T. Eaton department store. This was their first "talkie": the Marx Brothers in *Coconuts*. I always remember Groucho going down on his knees to a large, bosomy woman and saying, "Your eyes! They shine like the seat of my blue serge trousers."

When we came out we had to walk along Portage Avenue to the Hudson's Bay Company where our car was parked. We were embarrassed because our eldest son kept collapsing and doubling up with laughter as he and his brother repeated the lines which they appeared to have got verbatim.

This was early in September. In October the great depression got under way. I can remember the newsboy shouting at the corner of Portage and Main "Stock Market Crash! Stock Market Crash! Read all about it." It was a cold windy night, and I could feel the cold grip my heart. Bad times had come again.

And bad they were. In western Canada the basic cause of depression was low incomes which were in turn caused by the low world price of cereals and natural products and their short supply on the prairies caused by the drought. Each made the other harder to bear, and combined to drive incomes down below starvation levels in the driest and most wind blown areas of southeastern Alberta and southern Saskatchewan. The sufferers had no alternative but flight from what was becoming a desert terribly hot in summer and frozen solid in winter. They fled north and east to moister regions or to the cities in search of relief. Among my most vivid memories were two examples of families fleeing northward which I encountered while travelling on my work. One family had loaded all their possessions into a bundle wagon. Their horses pulled the wagon, their cow trailed behind at the end of rope tied to the back of the wagon, and their chickens were in crates on the top of their funiture. The father and mother sat in the front of the wagon, the bigger children walked and the smaller children dangled their legs from the edge of the vehicle. On one of the uprights of the wagon they had painted in whitewash "In God we trusted and now we're busted."

The other case was similar except that the family's conveyance was an ancient Ford truck on which they had inscribed the legend: "Hailed out, dried out, frozen out, getting out."

At that time the sky was darkened by clouds of dust as far

162

east as Manitoba, and even in Manitoba there were drifts of top soil on the road allowances and against the fence posts. And we used to see during more than one summer another kind of cloud in the sky: the humming silver cloud of grasshoppers. In an age of insecticides it is hard to make people believe what a plague of locusts is like. On one occasion I was visiting a farm at Pipestone, Manitoba. The farmer had a fine field of about twenty acres of oats just beginning to head. At breakfast he said to me: "The hoppers are near, and I'm going to cut that field of oats, and get it in for the cattle." He began to cut and rake, and the next day the grasshoppers were there stripping the stubble and going for the roots. Grasshoppers were voracious. I have seen them chew up corn stalks and hollow out turnips.

One of my wife's cousins who farmed a section at Riverhurst, Saskatchewan, only managed to stay and survive the drought because in an earlier time of prosperity during World War I he had sunk a deep well. This enabled him to water a garden and keep his animals alive. But he had to fight the insects. He dug a great trench around his garden, which filled with the army worms beseiging his place. Before they mounted the inner side of his defences he spread gasoline and burnt them out. He was lucky that his enemies were not air borne. Grasshoppers could not live in the drought on account of inadequate fuel supplies.

And yet it would be false to pretend that the bad times of the 1930's were bad times for me and my family. During the ten years between the onset of the depression and the outbreak of World War II two of our children graduated from the University of Manitoba, and two more were attending the University. We had some wonderful holidays on Lake Winnipeg and in the Lake of the Woods. We did not travel much outside Manitoba, but we did see a lot of that province. We ate well, and we enjoyed ourselves in spite of the disasters, scandals, social antagonisms and political uncertainty which Jimmy

Gray has so well and accurately described in *The Winter Years.*
And I should add that I was always busy at my job, had plenty
to do and I liked what I was doing.

There are two facts which explain the contrast between
the well being of me and my family and the surrounding mis-
ery and disorder which afflicted tens of thousands of people
in western Canada and many thousands in Winnipeg itself. The
first fact was a steady job with a steady income which was
only once reduced when the Bennett government cut the sal-
aries of the civil servants by 10% in 1934. The second was my
share in the work of an industry which grew during the depression as a result of people having to find alternative opportunities to grain farming and of the government opening up
markets for poultry, among other places, in the United Kingdom.

Our income remained a good deal steadier than the prices
of things we had to buy. Although my salary never exceeded
$2,000.00 a year, and our children never added significantly to
the family income because there were few or no vacation jobs
going, we were able to buy three pound blocks of butter in the
Eaton's Groceteria on North Main Street for as little as 33
cents; the finest fillets of pickerel out of Lake Winnipeg for
11—15 cents a pound. A good sized roast of beef cost 40—45
cents. A man's shirt could be bought for a dollar or less. A
good suit with two pairs of trousers could be purchased for as
little as $19.95 if one watched for the sales at Eaton's or the
Hudson's Bay, and one could clothe the family for a couple of
hundred dollars a year without resorting to cut price bargain
stores on Main Street south of the C.P.R. tracks. One could
buy a Model A Ford for less than $1,000 and could count on
6 or 7 years good service. Gas was 18—20 cents a gallon. A
beach cottage rented for $8—12 a week. The electricity for a
house cost $2—3 a month; a telephone was $1.50. Street car
fares were 2 for 15 cents and on a pass costing $5.00 one
could ride as much as one wanted for a month anywhere in
Winnipeg. When our elder son started to the University of

Manitoba the fees were $65 a year plus $5 for a student organization fee. After the robbery of the University's endowments was discovered in 1932 the fees were nearly doubled, almost the only price which went up in the 1930's.

When I suggest that we "had it good" during the depression I do not want the reader to think that we were wallowing in luxury or that any sane man would or could welcome a return to the 1930's. In fact what we achieved during the 1930's was the result of hard work and the habits of economy which any Canadian had to practise if they were to survive and prosper. This meant living simply and having no expensive vices. There was never a drop of alcohol in our house, and I smoked maybe ten cigarettes a week and occasionally had a glass of beer with friends when I was out working. I think it was 1936 before we had a radio with valves and a loud speaker fixed in a cabinet, although we had long had a crystal set with ear phones. It was seldom that the whole family ever went to the movies, and we never ate a meal in a restaurant, even though one could get a reasonable three course lunch in Moore's on Portage Avenue for 45 cents. The children sometimes went to matinees at the College Theatre on North Main Street, or to the Deluxe nearby or the Roxy in East Kildonan. It was a special treat for our children to go to a "feature" at any of the theatres downtown like the Metropolitan or the Capitol. My wife once took our eldest son to see Sir John Martin Harvey's production of *Hamlet* in the Walker Theatre and around 1935 I can remember hearing Yehudi Menuhin play the violin in the Civic Auditorium. But hearing Yehudi Menuhin or going to a Celebrity Concert were regarded as special events, because they really were special and seldom experienced. I can remember my second son asking in 1938 or 1939 "How can you have a girl on an allowance of $2.00 a week?" and I remember the reply of my wife, who managed the family budget, "Ask Harry. He managed on 75 cents a week." She was referring to the years of excessive depression in 1932 and 1933.

The worst aspect of the depression was what it did to

young people, especially those who tried to get some educattion. We knew one young fellow who graduated in engineering. His father was a high civic official who was supposed to have influence, but that boy never had a better job than selling sausages in Eaton's meat department until he joined the Air Force in 1939, where he was soon a Wing Commander. The best job another young man we knew in the North End, ever had in the 1930's was selling neck ties in Eaton's haberdashery department and yet he ended the war as a Brigadier in the army. Our eldest daughter considered herself lucky when she graduated in 1937. She got a job in an insurance office at $25 a month. There was a saying, "If you have a B.A. and a nickel you can get a cup of coffee just like anyone else."

The slavery which my wife had experienced in Strathmore was at an end, but this did not mean that she did not have to work hard. Hot and cold running water and electricity were the secret of her emancipation, but she still sewed, canned fruit, did all her own washing and cleaning, although assisted in this by an electric washing machine and an electric vacuum cleaner. My wife did all our interior decorating, and I painted our house. In 1930 I spent less than $25.00 for the materials to paint the house. In 1973 I paid $890.00 to have painted a house half the size of our house on Inkster Boulevard. Coal for heating the house was expensive and one could expect to burn up to 8 tons a year at $12.00 a ton. We economized on heating by having the house insulated. I insulated the house myself with wood shavings. I did this for about $40.00.

And that was how it was for those who were lucky enough to have jobs. I remember hearing how Friedel Simkin and his son, Dave, who ran the Universal Printers and Israelite Press on Selkirk Avenue East, used to allow themselves $10.00 a week each for living expenses through most of the 1930's. Dave became a very rich man before he died, lived on Wellington Crescent and financed a professional hockey team.

People sometimes ask me why, if things were so bad in Winnipeg in the 1930's, there was no revolution. Was this because there were just enough people like myself doing moderately well that we swung the balance in favour of the status quo? No. This is not the answer. I think the answer is this. Everybody was so busy with surviving that few people had the energy or the inclination to listen to pie in the sky schemes of solving all problems in one big sudden commotion. That never made sense. The people who had time on their hands to talk about such schemes and to listen to political oratory were not the practical people who get things done. Those who had the ability and the determination to do things found enough opportunities in adverse circumstances to accomplish the objective of surviving and even improving their lot. The result of this was, it seems to me, that a new life and way of doing things grew up in Manitoba that was not brought about by talk and street demonstrations. For most people I knew life was too serious for this sort of thing, and very few people took much notice of people like Mayor Ralph Webb who wanted to throw the reds in the Red River, nor did they take much notice of the reds who wanted to hang Webb and to bring in the millenium. People voted Bennett out in 1935 and Mackenzie King in for the same reason that Manitoba kept Bracken in office. The politicians who said least were the ones likely to interfere least with the business of surviving. That seems to me the long and short of it.

When I look back on those years I think Bennett did more good than he was given credit for. He handed out relief to people who were really down and out, but more important the government did something to repair the disasters brought on by ploughing up land in the Palliser Triangle and it opened up new markets for people like the poultry farmers, the hog breeders and the cattle feeders. In this way the producers in Manitoba and elsewhere in the West, who were willing to work instead of dreaming about the bonanza of a good crop, were able to get somewhere and make a living. That's my angle, and that is the angle from which I saw things as a part of the poultry industry.

167

During these years the promotion of the poultry industry by government schemes such as the R.O.P. began to pay off. By the 30's the idea of breeding poultry and not just keeping hens had taken a real hold on the farming community, and there had developed the means of implementing the idea. Take, for example, the hatching business. The fact that there were commercial hatcheries accustomed to hatching from eggs from good stock meant that anyone who was prepared to do a bit of work and use a bit of common sense based on suggestions anybody could pick up from publications, government pamphlets and talks by field men employed by the government or the big packing houses could by a small investment in stock and equipment become a producer with something to sell and so earn an income. One could see this happening everywhere in Manitoba, and not just in poultry. The Ottawa Agreements about marketing in Britain opened up new outlets and this encouraged people to produce more cheaply so that we could sell both at home and abroad in spite of low prices. Nobody was going to make a fortune, but a lot were going to make a living, and in the 1930's that was what people would settle for.

And it was not just the poultry farmers and hog breeders who benefited. The big packing plants were solidly behind the new development, for two reasons. In the first place there was a new and expanding line of business for them, and in the second, poultry raising opened up outlets for manufactured feeds like bone meal and protein foods. In the same way the milling companies were interested in and supported an industry which consumed more and more feed especially manufactured for poultry.

In order to understand the development of the agricultural industry in western Canada during the late 1920's, it is necessary to appreciate the role of the federal and provincial governments therein, and the leadership they, and particularly the federal government, gave in creating opportunities for farmers, merchants and food processors to produce more to sell more and to make a reasonable living by supplying Canada and the world with an important means of life. The first big fact is that neither the Federal nor the Provincial Governments ever thought of attempting to own anything, produce anything or sell anything. This was left to the farmers, the wholesalers and the processors. The role of the Government was to educate, to organize and to find markets outside Canada by negotiation with other governments. It also controlled production and marketing with the object of seeing that the people involved in production and consumption got a square deal. A square deal had little or nothing to do with prices. The square deal the government sought to achieve by control concerned the quality and reliability of the commodities which were traded; and not only the end commodity which the consumer purchased either in Canada or abroad. A good quality Canadian turkey sold in Liverpool, England, started as a good quality hatching egg in, say, Eriksdale, Manitoba. It was a good hatching egg because the man or more often the woman who owned the flock of turkeys knew how to keep them clean and healthy, knew how to breed and feed the turkeys. The hatchery which bought the turkey egg could be reasonably certain that it would hatch, and that the chick would grow up to be a bird suitable for sale. Why? Because a government inspector had blood tested the turkey flock for disease and had certified the ancestry of the bird. When it was killed and packed, a government inspector certified that the bird belonged to a general classification, Special, A, B, C or D, depending on weight, appearance, proportion of fat to flesh to bone, and so on, so that the buyer could buy with confidence without actually having to look at each bird or even look at a car load or a boat load. This is all the Government officials did, but what they did was important. And for this reason. Each participant in the process from first to last could get on with his job in the confidence that he or she was not being deceived or misled by someone falling down on their particular job because they were ignorant, lazy or crooked. Everybody likes to have an income, and the true business of government and the economic organization of society is to see that each income earner matches his or her income by a productive contribution to society. This is what the Government of Canada was doing with respect to agricultural production in the 1920's and 1930's, and I had a small part in this activity.

The man who did the most to make the role of government in the production of poultry in Manitoba a reality was my superior, A. C. McCulloch. Mac was essentially an educator and an organizer, and he and I saw eye to eye on what was needed to get things moving in that part of the agricultural business which was our concern. First there was education. In the 1920's Mac's principal brain child was the Manitoba Approved Flock. Put simply, Mac went around the province persuading farmers to cull their flocks of birds in order to select the ones likely to produce enough eggs to show a profit and to discard those which were unlikely to produce. In this way he interested those raising poultry in better breeding, and in turn built up systematic breeding through the R.O.P. system. But this involved more than eggs.

On the one hand it involved building up commercial and carefully managed hatching, and on the other of developing the technique of feeding, killing, dressing and selling the poultry used in egg production. It was Mac's concern with these aspects of the business which laid the foundation of the inspection system. Three or four years before Parliament legislated to establish the inspection of poultry and other livestock products Mac had established in Manitoba the outlines of the system and had persuaded a significant proportion of the farmers that the system would operate to the benefit of all, and was the way to produce more, to produce more cheaply and to produce a better and hence more saleable product. In 1930 Parliament passed the Livestock and Livestock Products Act which established the legal basis for the regulation of the poultry industry.

Mac did not limit himself to laying the foundations of a government operated system of quality control. He turned his attention to marketing. McCulloch was the real founder of the poultry pool—the Manitoba Poultry Marketing Association Ltd. This was a cooperative based on a simple principle. Each member paid an entrance fee of $1.00 and undertook to deliver all his produce to the Association, which would grade it, pack it, ship it and sell it, paying to the member a basic price and a share of the profits of the total operation. The members elected a board of directors who appointed a general manager.

McCulloch was the father of the Association, but the man who ran it was a farmer from Napinka, Manitoba, W. A. Landreth. He was not much of a farmer, but he was an excellent organizer, politician and business man. Just as sometimes happens between father and son there was no love lost between Mac and W. A. Landreth, but for many years they worked together and watched each other like fighting cocks. In fact, Landreth needed McCulloch and the services of the government and McCulloch needed Landreth to realize the objects of the government policies, of which Mac was in some degree the author. The fact that Landreth got more out of the venture in a material sense than McCulloch did not much affect their relationship. It is my observation that civil servants and politicians never get as much materially out of public activity as the business men who benefit by it. In a small way McCulloch did not differ from Sir John A. McDonald in a big way.

Every year from mid-October until mid-December everyone connected with the poultry business was involved in an intensive harvesting operation, which required much detailed planning and close cooperation between the Pool (as the Manitoba Poultry Marketing Association was customarily called), the Government services of which McCulloch and I were the principals, and the railways. Because the operation involved many people and was financed on a shoestring, cooperation and planning took the place of the capital equipment and managerial overheads of ordinary commercial enterprises. The October and November slaughter of poultry was destined for quick sale as a fresh product between mid-December and the first week in January in markets in the cities of Canada, and, after the Ottawa Agreements in 1932, in the British market. Maintenance of freshness depended on the weather at least until the cities or the transatlantic steamers were reached where the poultry could be chilled but not frozen until sold to the retailer. There were risks in this aspect of the operation, but they had to be taken and the weather of Manitoba seldom let us down in the matter of sufficiently low temperatures.

The whole operation was dependent on railways. Neither roads nor trucks were equal to the movement of produce in the 1920's and 1930's, except short distances, in and around Winnipeg or in transporting produce to loading points along the railway lines. These points were established and provided with packing boxes, and temporary accomodation for the buying, grading and packing operations were obtained. Teams of graders, packers and inspectors worked from depot to depot along the railway lines from the borders of Saskatchewan day by day towards Winnipeg. Every day was a long one, and few connected with the operation got much sleep for six weeks. After the whole operation Mac used to knock off to recuperate for a week. One experience of the packing season would soon dispel the notion that a government job was a sinecure.

The Pool was the principal agency in developing the market for poultry. As its operations developed the big packing houses, like Swifts Canadian and Canada Packers together with the small independents like Roy Calof's Dominion Poultry Sales and Joe Kershrot's Standard Produce got into the act. They, too, established depots and sought to compete with the Pool offering a slightly better cash price or easier grading. This was all to the good, for it kept the Pool on its toes and gave the producers no cause to kick. If they did not like the Pool, they could sell elsewhere and vice-versa.

It must not be supposed that Mac and I worked only in October, November and December. In the spring we had to attend to the growing hatchery business in order to fix standards and guarantee that those selling hatching eggs were getting a square deal and that the hatcheries themselves were getting a square deal from their suppliers of hatching eggs. If this could be insured there was a good chance that the purchasers of baby chicks or poults would also get a square deal. Underlying the square deal all around was the certifying of breeding stock which I have already described, and the blood testing of flocks, particularly of chicks, to ascertain the presence or absence of disease. In their natural state or in the pre-commercial age of poultry keeping, poultry diseases were present but poultry had their own ways of keeping healthy—eating, for instance, cow dung which is a specific against various infections. As flocks grew, however, the incidence of coccidiosis, an infection of the alimentary tract and chronic respiratory disease increased. Blood testing indicated the presence of such diseases, and this made possible the isolation of the diseases and their treatment. Above all it limited its transmission by keeping the eggs of infected flocks out of the hatcheries.

The regulatory aspect of our work, which had a police aspect and was backed up with the sanction of the law, depended not on the power of enforcement but upon the power of persuasion. Enforcement by prosecution was seldom effective. The provincial courts were not sympathetic, and one rascal in the hatchery business got himself out of trouble by political influence in Ottawa. But in any case legal sanctions were of limited value. What made the system work was the self evident advantage of the system to the people affected by it. I am convinced on the basis of my experience that laws and regulations only work well when they serve the interest of those affected, and where this is so only a very small percentage of fools and crooks ever take advantage of their fellow men and women. If one is engaged in an activity which involves work and the use of intelligence the presence of fools and crooks is minimal.

173

11

When the war came in 1939 the agricultural industry of western Canada was geared up for production. When I look back on it now I can see that the years of depression were years of fundamental change in which new ways of doing things and new people came to the fore and that in many ways the new society produced by the challenge of depression, if not better, was certainly stronger and more productive than that which had existed before World War I and in the 1920's. World War II did not much affect that part of the poultry business with which I was concerned. We just did more, but nothing essentially new. After the War until my retirement in 1954 I witnessed the beginning of the end of the industry as I had known it more than 35 years. Advances in the manufacture of motor trucks which could be insulated, refrigerated, heated and equipped with lifting devices together with the improvement of roads laid the foundations for more concentrated production of all poultry products in bigger units of production, handling and merchandizing. Technical development inside the industry itself pointed in the same direction; bigger and more automated poultry plants; bigger and more automated hatcheries; bigger and more automated plants for processing eggs and poultry; and finally bigger outlets in the form of supermarkets.

The role of the government services changed. No longer was it necessary to teach farm men and women how to cull flocks, breed and kill poultry, nor was it necessary to teach employees of the cooperative how to pack and present their product so it would be acceptable in the British market. The R.O.P. system was on the way out, dwindled steadily, and was wound up in 1964 after I retired. Breeding was ceasing to be an activity of a comparatively large number of small producers, working under government leadership and with government help; it was becoming a large scale, concentrated specialized activity in the hands of large enterprises which employed their own technically trained people who produced and sold to other specialists a tested product with specific qualities: either the capacity to lay eggs or to grow up quickly with flesh on the frame. The egg producers or broiler plants were capital-intensive using complicated equipment where poultry were automatically cleaned and so on. Production no longer followed seasonal cycles. For thousands of years poultry like other birds were born in the spring, came to maturity in the autumn, lived through the winter and bred in early spring. But not any longer. By the late 1950's the life cycle of poultry had been altered to meet the needs of the super markets. Breeding in the early spring was not even strictly for the birds. It happened also in the autumn in order to supply eggs and poultry the year round. About the only type of poultry which has managed to keep to the cycles of nature is the turkey, and this only because Christmas happens to fall in late December. At least the turkeys have been saved from science by religion.

What has been the value of the revolution I have briefly described? Certainly eggs and poultry have been produced more abundantly, and for many years during the 1950's and 1960's these products became cheaper and cheaper relative to other commodities and even in comparison with other foods so that eggs and poultry became one of the least expensive protein foods. Quality was better in terms of purity and the increased probability that the final purchaser could actually use and eat what he or she had purchased. But there were some losses, too: principally in flavour. Everything became bland, so that now practically no one knows what eggs or chicken can taste like. So much attention is paid to cleanliness and speed, that the bacteria which impart flavour and the outdoor life which develops fibre are gone. Chicken may be finger-lickin' good, but the taste comes from the finger and not from the chicken. We have now reached the point that existed in medieval times when the meat was so bad that it had to be disguised with spices. Our poultry is so good that it has to be disguised by the same means.

Retirement from the government service in 1954 did not mean for me the end of my connection with the poultry industry. Briefly I managed the R.O.P. Cooperative Hatchery in Winnipeg until my wife and I set out for our first visit to Europe. In 1956 I was appointed secretary-manager of the Manitoba Turkey Association, and continued in this office until January 1964. The turkey industry was one part of the poultry business which retained, as it still retains, some of the old characteristics of the poultry industry with which I had been familiar during my working life. The reasons for this are quite simple to state. Turkeys are produced for only one purpose: their flesh, and the market for turkeys is seasonal. Thus continuous demand is not a factor in altering the cycle of nature of turkeys themselves. They cannot be raised under confined industrial conditions. They more resemble cattle in their feeding habits and their need for an open life on a range. While there are advantages in keeping turkeys on a large scale and very few turkeys are now produced in small flocks as an adjunct to some other agricultural or even urban activity, the man or woman who raises turkeys commercially has to have an establishment more like the traditional farm or ranch where open space is available, where land is cultivated to provide the right kind of fodder for the birds, and where the birds themselves feed directly on growing plants. Like cattle, turkeys have been robbed of their sex life by artificial insemination and breeding is closely controlled as with other livestock, for the purpose of obtaining the right kind of product which the public will buy.

And so in working for the Manitoba Turkey Association I was working with and for farmers who had had all the problems of working separately as individual producers and at the same time working together to look after their interests and develop their businesses. The Association was in the main a pressure group whose purpose was to fight for its members not just in the competitive market but in the formation of the policies of the Government. The Association financed itself by a kind of tax on its members which we called the Centapoult, i.e. the payment of a contribution to the Association of one cent for each turkey which the farmers marketed each year. When I started as secretary-manager there was $40.00 in the Association's bank account, and there was $4000.00 there when I left. From these figures it was apparent that the Manitoba Turkey Association was never a well-heeled body.

Its real strength was its members. It was a recognized fact that turkeys as a product competed with other similar products such as beef, pork, lamb and other poultry and that this competition was not just about prices. Modern advertising and public relations activities being what they are it was quite possible for the advertising specialist active on behalf of other products to persuade the public that Thanksgiving, Christmas and New Years ought to be celebrated by serving fried balogna, and that turkey at the feast is no more a natural custom than the mini-skirt or the crew-cut. Our policy was to talk turkey and ask the question *parlez-vous de dindon?* with the object of preserving the custom so important to the livelihood of the turkey breeders. Of course, we were not content with preserving. Like business people everywhere the turkey producers wanted to grow and to expand. If the hamburger could have been displaced by the turkey burger as a universal food the turkey producers would have been supremely happy. Our limited resources were not only devoted to advertising—talking turkey— but were used to foster experimentation in ways to make turkey an everyday food and not just a Christmas treat.

Turkeys were bred to become smaller. They were cut up,

canned, compressed, ground, frozen, liquified, chilled and disguised all for the purpose of finding ways of opening up new markets and securing the expansion of the industry. The producers of other meats were doing the same thing, and I cannot record that the turkey interests did no more than hold their own against attempts to take over Christmas. In any case, it always seemed to me, that if the public was convinced that turkey was an ordinary food like sausages or hamburger it would cease to be regarded as a festive food, and people would begin to look more closely at the price than they did when they only made one or two purchases a year at a time when there was a strong traditional compulsion to buy and a not too well developed disposition to look at the cost.

Then there was the matter of the Americans. They had developed a large scale turkey industry, and there was always a danger that they might flood the Canadian market with their surpluses. The Manitoba Turkey Association in collaboration with the Canadian Poultry Products Institute had the job of keeping the politicians and bureaucrats in Ottawa alert to this danger and of lobbying on behalf of tariffs and/or subsidies to preserve us from the Americans. Of course, we agitated for action not only to keep the Americans out of our markets but to get into theirs. As the industry grew and techniques improved this was a natural demand. Everybody likes competition once they have a good chance of winning.

There was, of course, a social side to the Association. Turkey men and women liked to get together from time to time not just to discuss their interests and to play at the politics of deciding who has what office, but simply to eat, drink and gossip together. I used to organize barbecues here and there around the province of Manitoba usually on the farm of a big breeder or, on one occasion, at the University of Manitoba's poultry science plant. These were jolly affairs, and I got to be a fair chef in the very limited field of cooking turkeys out of doors.

By the end of 1963 I was more than seventy-five years

old and in any event I had ceased to see eye to eye with the leading producers themselves on two points. The first concerned finance. One or two of the big producers refused to pull their weight. I was obliged to spend a great deal of time persuading the small producers to pay the Centapoult levy of one cent a bird. The small producers did pay up, but some of the big operators seemed to think that a few hundred dollars was all they ought to contribute. And yet these very men were the ones most anxious to use the Association for purposes with which I could never agree, and this was the second of my reasons for wanting to quit. Some of the big operators wanted to stabilize the market; that is to cut production, fix prices and maximize their profits by means of a monopoly control backed up by government legislation of the marketing board type. This went against the grain for me. I could not bring myself to sympathize with and to support the people who wanted an easy life on the basis of controls which inevitably would prevent new men and women from entering the business and showing what they could do. In any case I believed that controls would never work effectively in an industry like the turkey business unless Canada ceased to be a free country. After all one aspect of liberty is the freedom to breed and sell turkeys, not perhaps the most important but real none the less. By the time of the annual general meeting of the Association in January 1964, the leaders knew pretty well how I felt and I was voted out of office. Since then I have been in real retirement.

These years of work after my retirement from the service of the Government of Canada were broken by one spell of travel outside of North America—my first. In 1955 my wife and I did something which millions of Canadians have done before and since. We made a journey to visit the graves of our ancestors to see what our begetters—friends and enemies alike —have done, and how they have expressed themselves in their buildings, wall paintings, music and entertainment and to see

179

how our cousins by many removes are behaving themselves in the last half of the twentieth century.

I found travel to Europe rewarding in the sense that it gave me a means of looking at my own life and my own country from a new angle. In Britain, France, Switzerland and Italy I found societies which no one from North America could despise. On the other hand, I did feel after it was all over that we need not despise ourselves either. As far as natural scenery and accommodation for travellers, Europe has different experiences to offer but not better ones. On the other hand I found that my brief experience in Europe did something for me which I wish I had more life left to develop.

Take for example music. From the time I was quite small and sang in the choir of Cronyn Memorial Church in London, I always liked music and, as I have already related, I used to get a very great deal of pleasure going to the musical road shows and light operas which stopped off at the Grand in London. But what I felt obliged to like were the musical comedies such as *Chu Chin Chow,* or *The Quaker Girl* and things like that. It was not the thing to admire grand opera or what is called good music or the theatre of Shakespeare etc. A whole range of entertainment was regarded as boring, snobbish upper class stuff which no he-man could or ought to enjoy. I shared this popular view, but the "serious stuff" always had a secret, sneaking attraction for me. I once had a friend in Calgary with whom I roomed for a time, Archie Still, who had a piano and knew a lot about music. He was the only man I ever knew intimately who was prepared to say that good music is good music and is worthy of appreciation. He used to lend me books, and I would have read them more completely than I did, had I not been so busy bricklaying, speculating in land and chasing after big money.

In Britian and on the continent of Europe I found the good stuff in abundance and no one needed to keep quiet about liking it. What disappointed me is that I did not really know enough to take it all, or even very much of it, in. But

I sensed that there was something there which secretly I had always admired and longed for. The best word I can use to name it is magnificence.

Take Chatsworth for example. That is the home of the Duke of Devonshire in Derbyshire in England. It is, of course, a house and a garden in the same sense that where I live in Winnipeg is a house and a garden or where a millionaire may live is a house and a garden. But there is something extra at Chatsworth. It is not merely bigger. Its furniture is not merely more lush and expensive. The Duke of Devonshire has not merely more knick-knacks and curious odds and ends than the richest Canadian. No. Chatsworth is different. It has what I call magnificence, which, over-all, cannot be bought. You can buy the parts, but nobody can buy it as a whole.

The same goes for a great many of the churches, and it is not just a matter of being old or big or highly decorated. Take the example of Lincoln Cathedral or Santa Maria Maggiore in Rome. They have that extra dimension. They create in me the same sense of magnificence that I experience when I look at a great power dam in Canada. This may sound funny, but I think that a big power dam like that at Seven Sisters or Shipshaw has that something extra that is beyond the capacity of the individual or even a group of individuals; the work of men, yes, but something beyond them.

Of course much of our travel in Britain and Europe was intended for purposes other than standing in awe. We hired a car in England, and kept off the main roads. We saw some wonderful country—hand made country unlike what we have in Canada except here and there in the long settled parts. We travelled before the hotel keepers of England thought much about modernizing and so we encountered, for example, sanitation superior to what we had in Strathmore, Alberta, but primitive by the standards of Toronto or Winnipeg. But we found cleanliness and comfort and good food. I think we had only one bad meal—at Wisbech in Cambridgeshire. Of course we visited Rutlandshire whence came some of my family. We

181

went on to visit the places whence my wife's family came: Sutton le Marsh in Lincolnshire, where my wife's mother was born. At Outwell we found a grave yard where there were buried many people of the name of Trott, my wife's mother's name. Then we went to Devonshire, whence her father came and where some of her cousins still lived: Torrington, in north Devon where her father was born; Northam where a cousin lived and Torquay, where two more cousins lived in a large house.

We spent some time in old London. This is, of course, a town of endless interest, and I do not intend to write endlessly about it. One thing about London that I liked was the fact that unlike all Canadian cities it has no centre; no downtown. London had many centres: the City, Bloomsbury, Chelsea, Kensington, Soho, and so on, all different so that in London you are in several cities running into one another. Another thing which interested me was the question of how and why such large areas as Hyde Park, St. James's Park and Kensington Gardens right in the heart of one of the biggest cities in the world could have been saved for hundreds of years from land speculators and people which we call today developers. It is my experience that land sooner or later gets taken over by someone or other for a profit, and the public as a whole seldom wins. This has not happened in London insofar as Hyde Park, Kensington Gardens etc. have been concerned. Look what happens so often in North America. In New York, Central Park has been taken over by the hoodlums, muggers and thugs, and there might now be some advantage in selling it to land speculators.

Of all the things we saw in London, the most wonderful to me was the Chelsea Flower Show. The English are incomparable gardeners, and this show is one of incredible magnificence and variety. If you judge a society by what it can do, then to me Britain is still tops. Apart from the flowers, another aspect of the show which was new to me and very impressive was the capacity for crowd control. In Canada I do not suppose more than 10,000 people ever assemble for any purpose except when strung out on the pavement to see the Stampede parade in Calgary or something of that kind. At the Chelsea Flower Show a hundred thousand, or so it seemed to me, moved about in an orderly way, saw what they wanted to see and fed and watered themselves without any serious inconvenience.

Some of our travel in Britain was all our own in a rented car and in keeping with our ideas of where we wanted to go and what we wanted to see. On the continent of Europe we put ourselves in the hands of tour operators largely because we did not know French or Italian or German and because we did not want the strain of finding our own hotels, etc. We traded ease for the opportunity to get on more intimate terms with the places we visited and this, perhaps, was a disadvantage and loss. But it had one gain, at least for me. I got to know people from Australia, New Zealand, South Africa and a few Americans in a way which would not otherwise have been possible. In spite of differing accents and differing climates I found that we all had similar experiences of life. This was a real bond, and we all talked the same language, not just English, but the same language of life. As far as I am concerned the Commonwealth is a reality even though the politicians say it is gone forever. After nearly twenty years we still exchange greetings with some of the people we met on tour in 1955.

Our first visit overseas was the best. We went again in 1959 and in 1968 to the wedding of one of our grandsons. By 1959 and certainly by 1968 Britain was changing, and not always for the better. Nastiness seemed to be getting the upper hand in people and things. But that's only the opinion of an outsider and an old one at that.

12

At the beginning of this book I described myself as a Canadian and member of the Ferns-Dickens tribe. I have not so far made anything but passing references to my own family: my wife and children. In fact my wife and family explain all else. It has been for them and with them that I have worked and survived.

It is hard to remember the time when I did not know my wife. As children we lived but two city blocks apart. In London, however, city blocks were large areas, and as small children we seldom wandered so far from our homes. Our playmates lived within a small radius—most of them on either side of William Street. My earliest remembrance of my wife's family, the Sings, concerns the funeral of their daughter —Lottie. I can still see the little white hearse used at that time when children were buried. I was one of a group of curious kids who watched at a distance as the little coffin was taken from the Sing family home at 708 Maitland Street. I first encountered my wife, Janie Sing, at St. George's School and in the Sunday School of Cronyn Memorial Church where we were both baptized and confirmed, and where eventually we were married. When I was a paper boy her family were customers of mine, but when I left home for Algoma in 1901 we never corresponded. After my return from the bush and during my spell in the grocery trade we began to go out together. We were at the stage of sweet sixteen. The high point in my life until that date was the time when I took Janie Sing to see

The Bonny Briar Bush, a popular melodrama presented by a travelling theatre company at the Grand Theatre. Janie's father was a building contractor, and she had some influence in persuading me to become a bricklaying apprentice, an otherwise unlikely trade for me, except that it involved work out of doors which I liked more than work like my father's and brothers'. When I went to the harvest fields Janie and I corresponded. When I was injured in December, 1905, her family sent me flowers when I was in the hospital and this moved me greatly. During my apprenticeship with Ed Martin we used to go to church together. Janie went to Toronto to work as a secretary, but by then we were unofficially engaged. How beautiful she looked in her white dress on the day she was confirmed. A picture of her then is still my most valued possession. She returned from Toronto on account of an illness and we became engaged. But we did not marry. I went away to the United States and on to Western Canada to establish myself and with the apparent success I have already described.

I have no doubt at all that my marriage to Janie Sing was the best thing I ever did, and that without her I could never have survived the hazards of my life. I was buffeted about, a victim of my own innocence, folly, circumstances and the kind of society in which I lived. I know I was on the skids more than once, but for my wife I am sure I would have skidded to oblivion. As it was I had the incentive to survive and I was helped to survive not just because my wife was a hard worker with a constant purpose but because she always stood by me. Loyalty of another human being is as important for survival and life as economic help, and that is what my wife gave me.

Then we had five children. These meant everything to both of us. My great regret is that I never knew my children when they were small as well as I would have liked. I was always working and preoccupied or I was travelling on the job away from home weeks and sometimes for months at a time. None the less our children were the purpose of our lives, and Janie and I both believed that our children ought to have a better education than we had had. By this we meant that they ought to go to High School and if possible to university. The educational opportunities of our children were always a factor in our decisions about where we would live and how we spent our money.

Of course parents may have plans for their children and children may differ with them about these. None of our children, however, seriously disagreed with the notion that education is desirable and to be preferred to the immediate delights of freedom and a job of one's own. I cannot remember any of them refusing to go to school, or to finish High School or not wanting to go to university. As it was they all went to St. John's Technical High School in Winnipeg and all graduated from the University of Manitoba: three in arts, one in commerce and one in home economics. Four of them successfully worked for post graduate degrees. One became an M.A. of Queen's University and an M.A. and Ph.D. of the University of Cambridge; another earned a Diploma in Social Work and an M. A. of the University of Manitoba; another a C.A. with Price Waterhouse at the University of Manitoba and another a Diploma in Education of the University of Manitoba. On the basis of this education one is a university professor in England; one is a high ranking provincial civil servant; one is a business man successful enough to retire into farming; one was a dietician before marriage and the fifth a high school teacher before marriage.

A willingness to seek education has persisted in our fourteen grandchildren. Our eldest grandson graduated with a good degree from Oxford University and, after returning to Canada, he earned an M.A. and Ph.D. at the University of Western Ontario. His brother graduated from Cambridge University with a first class in economics and an M.A. in sociology from the University of Birmingham. He, too, returned to Canada where he runs, in partnership with another ex—C.B.C. man, a T.V. production and equipment company in Toronto. His brother won all the prizes at University College, London, England, and is now a post-graduate student at the University of London. Our eldest grand-daughter graduated from the University of British Columbia. One of her sisters graduated from Acadia University and is now at the University of Saskatchewan. Another grand-daughter graduated from McGill, another from the University of Winnipeg. Only one grandchild so far has bypassed university for marriage and one proposes to go directly into training as a nurse. The rest are either at school or university somewhere in Canada. Of our great grandchildren it is too soon to speak.

Graduation from universities is not necessarily an indicator of a useful and worthwhile life, although it suggests more possibility of such a life than the youthful enemies of education are wont to assert. In the case of our children and our grandchildren their contribution to society seems to me positive and valuable. Our eldest son has written four books. One, *The Age of Mackenzie King,* written in collaboration with a former student, punctured some of the myths about the Liberal ascendency in Ottawa, and helped to initiate the shift of opinion which produced the Diefenbaker landslide. His three books on Argentina have been widely read in that country, and a Spanish translation of his book *Britain and Argentina in the Nineteenth Century* was the best selling book of non-fiction in Buenos Aires for six months after its publication. After a rocky time in Canada between 1940 and 1949 he migrated to England, where he has become the first professor and head of the department of political science of the University of Birmingham and was elected the Dean of his Faculty for a three year term extended to a fourth year. He is the author of the idea of an independent university in Britain and his name appears in the British *Who's Who* on account of his contribution to education and civic life in Britain.

Our eldest daughter has been a social worker in Winnipeg and has held many responsible offices in the civil service of the Province of Manitoba. She was for many years the Financial

Director of Social Aid Programmes of the province. She has long played an active role in the religious and educational work of the Anglican Church and particularly of St. John's Cathedral. Her private life has been as devoted as her work for public authorities, and my wife and I owe more to our daughter than it is easy to state.

Our second son served in the Canadian Army overseas. After the war he trained as a chartered accountant and entered the oil business. For some years until he retired in 1973 he was vice president and general manager of Canadian Propane Consolidated Ltd. Like many other Canadians he is fascinated by a return to an earlier epoch in Canadian life. He has taken over a near derelict farm in the Okanagan Valley in British Columbia, where he proposes to re-live the homestead experience—or as much of it as it is possible to do with money in the bank.

Our second daughter won prizes at the University. She trained as a dietician at the Ottawa Civic Hospital, and then worked at the Deer Lodge Hospital in Winnipeg and in the University of Manitoba until she married an engineer whose parents had come from Finland to settle at Pointe de Bois, Manitoba. She and her husband have lived in the province of Quebec since their marriage. Her husband manages a large manufacturing enterprise in Quebec. They have both become French-speaking Canadians, made so by social experience and not by birth.

Our youngest daughter was a school teacher until her marriage to a clergyman of the United Church. They have lived in several towns of Manitoba and in the city of Winnipeg. In 1971 her husband gave up the ministry and embarked on a career in business.

And so there is no longer a tribe. Its members are scattered across the country and outside it. I look at my great grandchildren and there I see eternal life. But as we have known and have been told for 3,000 years there is also the possibility of perishing in fire. And the possibility is now physical as well as moral. Life is an open question; as open as it was for me 85 years ago.